Dealing with Diversity

TELECLASS STUDY GUIDE

Second Edition

J. Q. Adams, Ph. D.
Associate Professor of Educational Foundations
Department of Educational Foundations
Western Illinois University
Macomb, Illinois 61455

Sponsored by:

The Board of Governors Universities

Member Institutions are:

Chicago State University
Eastern Illinois University
Governors State University
Northeastern Illinois University
Western Illinois University

Produced by:

Governors State University
University Park, Il 60466

 KENDALL/HUNT PUBLISHING COMPANY
4050 Westmark Drive   Dubuque, Iowa 52002

ACKNOWLEDGEMENTS

The producers wish sincerely to thank the following individuals:

Advisory Committee members:

Dr. Bartley McSwine, Chicago State University
Dr. David Ainsworth, Governors State University
Dr. Craig Eckert, Eastern Illinois University
Dr. Mary Ann Schwartz, Northeastern Illinois University
Ms. Carol Lanning, Board of Governors Universities System Office

Teleclass students:

Irene Broughton   Nory Kasprisin
Donna Cobb   Belinda Martin
Janet Cowser   Pat McQuarrie
Joe Crawford   Chris McAfee
Rosalinda Cruz   Joseph Talluto
Sally Giffney   Shirlee Trevison
Joyce Granderson   Susan Vorwerk
Julie Gude

And the faculty and staff of the:

Division of Humanities and Social Sciences
College of Arts and Sciences
Governors State University
Dr. Roger K. Oden, Chairperson

COURSE CONTENT

COURSE CONTENT

COURSE CONTENT

Course Description

"The Commission on Minority Participation in Education and American Life, One Third of a Nation," produced by the American Council on Education and the Education of the States, states that by the year 2000 one-third of the population of the U.S. will be nonwhite Americans or persons of color. This shift in demographics is compounded by the increase of other definable groups such as the disabled, the aged, gays and lesbians as well as a variety of other special interest groups. Given this growing human mosaic, every aspect of our society will be challenged by this new diversity. Hostile incidents targeting racial groups, women, and homosexuals abound on university campuses across the nation, and at election time referenda on the rights of gays are becoming more and more common. In addition, the ever-increasing internationalization of commerce puts Americans in direct competition with people who represent diverse ethnic, linguistic, religious, cultural, and racial populations.

This course has been developed to help you recognize and appreciate the differences and similarities between diverse groups and individuals in our multicultural society. It is our hope that armed with this knowledge, you will be able to make a difference and become a facilitator in improving intercultural relations.

Expected Student Outcomes

At the end of this course you should be able to:

1. recognize the societal implications of our nation's changing demographics,
2. demonstrate the importance of understanding and respecting cultural differences, and
3. work effectively to promote intercultural awareness between different groups and among individuals within these groups.

Required Readings

Rosenblum, K. E. and Travis, T. C. (1996). *The Meaning of Difference: American Constructions of Race, Sex and Gender, Social Class, and Sexual Orientation*. The McGraw-Hill Companies, New York. ISBN 0-07-053962-6

Course Structure

The videotapes are conducted in lecture/discussion style, with a live in-studio interactive student audience. They also feature guest experts and are supplemented with previously videotaped interviews and case study documentaries.

How to Use this Study Guide

This Student Study Guide is designed to assist you throughout this course. Each class is summarized with key concepts, reading assignments, and discussion questions. The guide also includes the graphics you will see on the screen so that you don't have to spend time copying them. Be sure to follow the study guide before viewing each tape in order to maximize your understanding of the class content.

DEALING WITH DIVERSITY — CLASS 1
Introduction to Culture and Diversity

I. INTRODUCTION

In the first class of this course we will explore our own individual ethnic/racial, religious, and cultural backgrounds. It is very important that we understand our own cultural backgrounds and origins in order to help us understand the differences and similarities between the diversity of individuals and groups in our society. In order to accomplish this you will observe the teleclass students participating in an exercise called, "Who in the World is in Here?" Be sure to record the various backgrounds of each student so that you can make inferences about the diversity of the students in the teleclass. For example, what continents do the majority of the students come from? What religions are not represented?

We will also learn a number of definitions which it will be necessary for you to master in order to have a foundation for understanding this material.

Before you watch the videotape for this lesson:
READ: "Framework Essay" in *The Meaning of Difference*, pages 1-34. Glossary of Terms located at the end of this Study Guide.

II. VIDEO INSERTS

There are two video inserts in the first class. The first insert is a video montage of cultural diversity in and around the Chicago, Illinois area. As you watch this insert consider the following questions:

A. What are some of the cultural images that stand out in the video montage?

B. If you had to draw a picture of what an American looks like based on this video montage what would this image look like? What are some of the difficulties that you might encounter trying to accomplish this?

The second video insert is an interview with Ms. Constance Potter, a microfilm researcher at the National Archives in Washington D.C. After you watch this insert consider the following questions:

A. What are some of the groups in the U.S. who find it difficult to trace their ancestry? Explain some of the limitations on utilizing the files and records at the National Archives?

B. What are some of the ways in which an individual can come into the U.S. undocumented?

III. GRAPHICS

As you watch the videotape, a number of important concepts will be discussed or presented in graphic illustrations. The most important concepts will be reproduced below in this section of the Study Guide while the others will be found in the Glossary at the back of the Study Guide. I would encourage you to use the space in the Study Guide to take notes on the presentations and discussions you observe in the videotape.

> **Culture –**
> The cognitive rules for appropriate behavior (including linguistic behavior) which are learned by people as a result of being members of the same group or community.

> **Macroculture –**
> The predominant core culture of a society. Even though the U.S.A. has been influenced by a number of microcultures it is probably most characterized by its WASP Traits.

> **Microculture –**
> Cultures that consist of unique institutions, values and cultural elements that are non-universalized and are shared primarily by members of specific cultural groups.

Ethnic Group –
A microcultural group or collectivity that
shares a common history and culture, common
values, and behaviors.

Ethnocentrism –
A tendency to view alien cultures with disfavor
and a resulting sense of inherent superiority.

Race –
An invalid paradigm developed by people to
justify the different treatments accorded to
different people. The classification systems
range from 3 to 32 races.

Egocentrism –
A tendency to view one's inherent qualities as
superior to any other individual(s) one comes
in contact with.

Paradigm –
A conceptual model that serves as a cognitive
map to organize experience so that it has meaning
and is comprehensible to the observer.

Status Mobility System –
The socially or culturally approved strategy for
getting ahead within a given population or society.

IV. REVIEW QUESTIONS

Now that you have studied the terms in the Glossary and viewed the videotape you should answer the following questions to make sure you understand the key concepts presented in this class.

1. What is your ancestry? From what cultures do your ancestors originate? To the best of your knowledge when did your first ancestors arrive in North America?

2. Compare and discuss some of the inferences the teleclass students made with your own inferences from the "Who in the World is in Here?" exercise.

3. What is the difference between a macroculture and a microculture? Give examples of how both macrocultures and microcultures influence each other in U. S. society.

4. What is the danger of groups or individuals being viewed from either an egocentric or ethnocentric perspective?

5. Discuss the difference between an essentialist and a constructionist viewpoint with regard to the concepts of race, class, and gender as described in the first framework essay in Section One, Constructing Categories of Difference, in *The Meaning of Difference*.

V. SUGGESTED ADDITIONAL BACKGROUND MATERIALS

Samovar, L. A. and Porter, R. E. (1991). *Intercultural Communication, A Reader*. Wadsworth Publishing Company. Belmont, CA.

Samovar, L. A. and Porter, R. E. (1991). *Communication Between Cultures*. Wadsworth Publishing Company. Belmont, CA.

Zaitchik, J., Roberts, W., and Zaitchik, H. (1994). *Face to Face: Readings on Confrontation and Accommodation in America*. Houghton Mifflin Company. Boston, MA.

DEALING WITH DIVERSITY — CLASS 2
Social Interaction in Diverse Settings: The SIM's Model

I. INTRODUCTION

In this class we will learn how to use a social interaction model that will help shape our understanding of how humans differ and yet are similar at the same time. This model features five major components that are overlapping and interdependent upon each other. The language we will learn to operationalize this model will carry over in all of the remaining classes for this course. In essence this model and its vocabulary will give us a kind of common language and perspective in which to describe and explore the various issues we will encounter throughout this course.

Before you watch the videotape for this lesson:
READ: Understanding Social Interaction in Culturally Diverse Settings: In *Multicultural Education: Strategies for Implementation in Colleges and Universities*. Reprinted in the Appendix by permission of the Illinois Staff and Curriculum Developers Association.

II. GRAPHICS

At this stage we suggest you watch the videotape. The graphics you will see on the screen are reproduced below to save you the trouble of copying them down. You might like to add your own comments as you watch the tape.

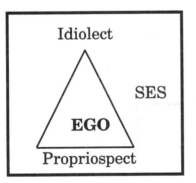

Propriospect –
The sum total of an individual's experiences
that enable him/her to make him/herself
intelligible to others.

Culture –
The cognitive rules for appropriate behavior
(including linguistic behavior) which are learned
by people as a result of being members of the same
group or community.

5

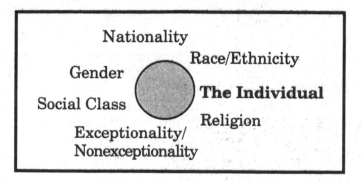

Nationality

Race/Ethnicity

Gender

The Individual

Social Class

Religion

Exceptionality/
Nonexceptionality

Idiolect –
An individual's unique system of articulation.
No two speakers operate a language in the
"same" manner.

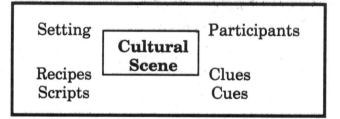

Setting

Participants

Cultural Scene

Recipes
Scripts

Clues
Cues

Cultural Scene –
The information shared by two or more people that
defines some aspect of their experience. Cultural
scenes are closely linked to recurrent social situations.

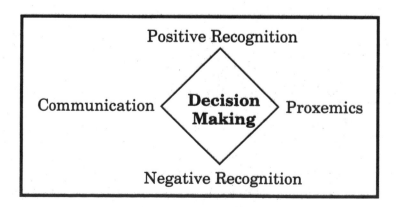

Positive Recognition

Communication

Decision Making

Proxemics

Negative Recognition

Aggregation –
The voluntary clustering by race or ethnicity
or class. Seating aggregation can be an index
for assessing student attitudes about interracial
and inter-ethnic contact.

Social Distance Model

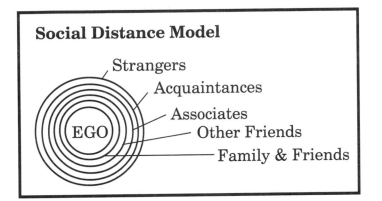

Strangers
Acquaintances
Associates
Other Friends
Family & Friends
EGO

Event Familiarity

Novice   Expert

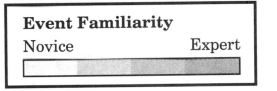

Event Familiarity –
The amount of general knowledge individuals bring
to a specific Cultural Scene based on their propriospect
which is necessary for accurate prediction of the event
scenario and appropriate behavior.

Understanding –
The individual's ability to intepret the cultural scene
and activate the appropriate script/recipe to respond
within the range of socially acceptable behavior.

III. REVIEW QUESTIONS

Now that you have completed the readings and viewed the videotape you should answer the following questions to make sure you understand the key concepts presented in this class.

1. Watch the opening video insert from Class 1 and utilize the SIM's model to describe any of the cultural scenes in the video.

2. Given your knowledge of the SIM's model describe a cultural scene that is occuring in your dorm, club, organization, or other social interaction opportunity.

3. Reconstruct the model by memory and write the correct definition for each of the major concepts.

IV. SUGGESTED ADDITIONAL BACKGROUND MATERIALS

Nelson, K. (1986). *Event Knowledge*. Lawrence Erlbaum Associates. Hillsdale, NJ.

Schank, R.C. and Ableson, R. P. (1977). *Scripts, Plans, Goals, and Understanding*. Lawrence Erlbaum Associates. Hillsdale, NJ.

DEALING WITH DIVERSITY — CLASS 3
Cross Cultural Communication in Diverse Settings

I. INTRODUCTION

In this class we will probe the difficulties of communicating accross cultures. We will begin with a basic understanding of communication by examining the characteristics and elements of communication. To help you understand the complexities of this subject matter our special guest for this class is Ms. Becky Parker, a professor of Speech Communication at Western Illinois University.

The class contains a variety of personal stories in communication, some humorous and some serious. As you listen to these illustrations think about similar events that may have happened to you.

 Before you watch the videotape for this lesson:
READ: 34: "Racism in the English Language," in *The Meaning of Difference*, pages 413-420.

II. GRAPHICS

 At this stage we suggest you watch the videotape. The graphics you will see on the screen are reproduced below to save you the trouble of copying them down. You might like to add your own comments as you watch the tape.

> **International Contacts**
> (Global Village)
> ■ Technology
> ■ Population
> ■ Economics

> **Macroculture –**
> The predominant core culture of a society.
> Even though the U.S.A. has been influenced
> by a number of microcultures, it is probably
> most characterized by its WASP traits.

> **Microculture –**
> Cultures that consist of unique institutions, values,
> and cultural elements that are nonuniversalized and are
> shared primarily by members of specific cultural groups.

**All Communication Involves
Six Basic Ingredients**

1. A **source** which
2. **encodes** an internal state into
3. a **message** that
4. travels by a **channel** to
5. a **receiver** which
6. **decodes** the message into a usable form.

Communication Elements

Perception:
- attitudes, beliefs, & values
- ethnocentrism
- world view
- social organization

Verbal processes:
- verbal language
- patterns of thought
- code-switching

Communication Elements

Nonverbal processes:
- nonverbal behavior
- space
- time

Communication context:
- high context cultures
- low context cultures

Characteristics of Communication

- no direct mind-to-mind contact
- we can only infer
- communication is symbolic
- time-binding links us together
- we seek to define the world
- has a consequence
- dynamic
- contextual
- rule-governed
- self-reflective

> **Greeting Sequences**
> – male to female
> – age
> – status
> – proxemics
> – race/ethnicity

III. REVIEW QUESTIONS

Now that you have completed the readings and viewed the videotape you should answer the following questions to make sure you understand the key concepts presented.

1. Name the six basic ingredients of communication.

2. What are some of the factors that culture imposes for effective communication across cultures?

3. Describe and discuss the communication elements of perception and verbal processes.

4. List at least three reasons why cross-cultural communication will become increasingly more important in the 21st Century.

5. Give at least three examples from the article, "Racism in the English Language," that illustrate how certain commonly used words or phrases can be demeaning to some groups in our society.

IV. SUGGESTED ADDITIONAL BACKGROUND MATERIALS

Delgado-Gaitan, C., and Trueba, H. (1991). *Crossing Cultural Borders: Education for Immigrant Families in America*. Philadelphia: Falmer Press.

Hall, E. T. (1976). *Beyond Culture*. Garden City, New York: Anchor Press/Doubleday.

Samovar, L. E. and Porter, R. E. (1991). *Intercultural Communication: A Reader*. 6th Edition. Belmont, Calif: Wadsworth.

Samovar, L. E. and Porter, R. E. (1991). *Communication Between Cultures*. Belmont, Calif: Wadsworth.

DEALING WITH DIVERSITY — CLASS 4
Global and National Demographic Trends

I. INTRODUCTION

This class concentrates on the rapidly changing demographic trends in the United States and around the world. In the first part of the class we will examine the changes in world population by continent over the past ten years. There will also be a discussion of major world religions and their distribution in North America. In the second part, the class discusses the population projections for the United States into the 21st century using data from both the 1980 and 1990 census. You should understand the impact of these population trends on the major ethnic groups in this country as well as the political, economic, and social implications they will likely have on our nation. When we add the discussion of the push - pull effect on migration from Asia, Europe, South and Central America we will be able to understand some of the major reasons behind these population trends.

Also covered in this class is an examination of Family Income by Education & Race. Be sure to understand such concepts as the "glass ceiling" effect and the changes in the American family.

Before you watch the videotape for this lesson:
READ: 28: "Making Sense of Diversity: Recent Research on Hispanic Minorities in the United States" in *The Meaning of Difference*, pages 330-336.

II. GRAPHICS

At this stage we suggest you watch the videotape. The graphics you will see on the screen are reproduced below to save you the trouble of copying them down. You might like to add your own comments as you watch the tape.

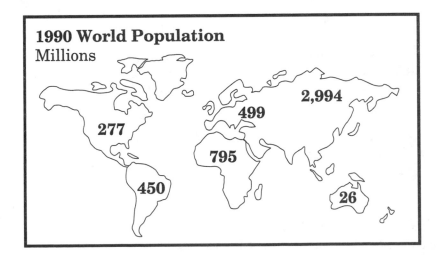

1990 World Population
Millions

277

499

2,994

795

450

26

World Population
Percents

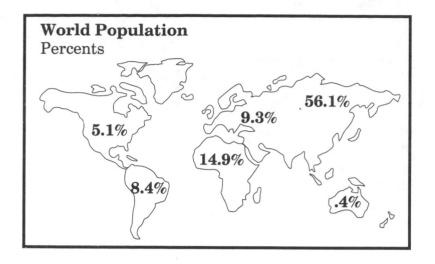

Major World Religions (Millions)

	North America	World	% World
Christians	235.0	1,758.7	36.3
Muslims	5.6	935.0	19.3
Hindus	1.25	705.0	14.5
Buddhist	.55	303.0	6.3
Jews	6.9	17.4	.4
Baha'is	.36	5.3	.1
Other	.48	17.9	.4
Atheist	1.3	233.0	4.8
Non-Religious	22.1	866.0	17.9

Projected U.S. Population
Number in Millions

Group	1980	2000	2020
White	181.0	200.3	205.6
Black	26.5	36.4	44.4
Hispanic	14.6	30.3	46.6
Asian/Other	4.4	12.1	20.3
Total U.S. **Population**	**226.5**	**279.1**	**316.9**

Projected U.S. Population
Percent of Total

Group	1980	2000	2020
White	79.9	71.9	64.9
Black	11.7	13.0	14.0
Hispanic	6.4	10.8	14.7
Asian/Other	2.0	4.3	6.4
Total U.S. Population	**100.0**	**100.0**	**100.0**

Population by Race
1990 Percentages

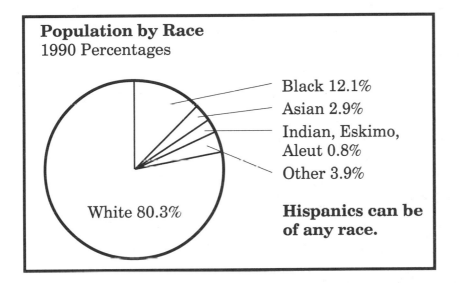

Black 12.1%

Asian 2.9%

Indian, Eskimo, Aleut 0.8%

Other 3.9%

White 80.3%

Hispanics can be of any race.

Population by Race
Growth since 1980

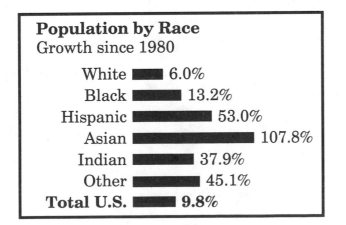

White ▬ 6.0%
Black ▬ 13.2%
Hispanic ▬ 53.0%
Asian ▬ 107.8%
Indian ▬ 37.9%
Other ▬ 45.1%
Total U.S. ▬ **9.8%**

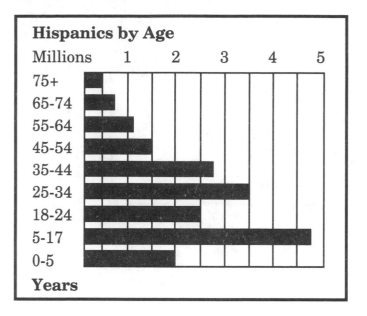

Hispanics by Age

Millions	1	2	3	4	5
75+					
65-74					
55-64					
45-54					
35-44					
25-34					
18-24					
5-17					
0-5					

Years

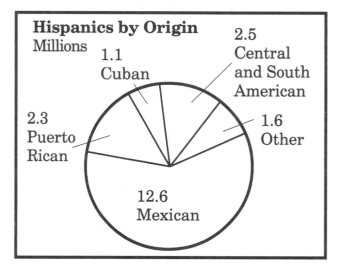

Hispanics by Origin
Millions

1.1 Cuban

2.5 Central and South American

2.3 Puerto Rican

1.6 Other

12.6 Mexican

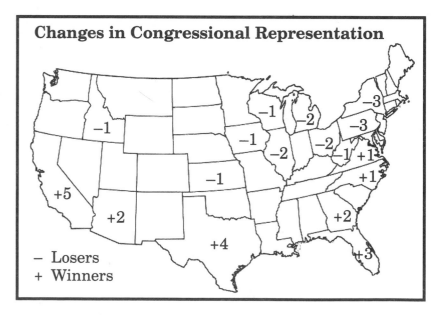

Changes in Congressional Representation

– Losers
+ Winners

Family Income by Education and Race for 1984			
School	**White**	**Black**	**Hispanic**
Under 8	$17K	$14K	$17K
8	22	15	19
9-10	24	16	19
12	30	21	26
College	35	23	30
BA/BSC	50	37	42
Graduate	54	42	45

III. CLASS REVIEW

Now that you have completed the readings and viewed the videotape for this class you should answer the following questions to make sure you understand the key concepts presented in this class.

1. What is the current population of the world? List the major geographical areas with the largest population to the smallest.

2. List the largest major world religions and contrast the global percentages to that of their representation in North America.

3. Describe some of the forces that are impacting the growth of ethnic/racial groups in the population of the United States.

4. What are some of the implications that this rapidly changing population will have on politics, education, and other facets of life in this country?

5. Discuss some of the reasons why the Hispanic population is growing so much faster than some of the other ethnic/racial groups.

6. Explain why there are differences in the family incomes of ethnic/racial groups even though they may have the same educational attainment.

7. Discuss the differences in education, occupation, and income among Spanish-Origin Groups found in Table 1 in the article "Making Sense of Diversity: Recent Research on Hispanic Minorities in the United States."

IV. SUGGESTED ADDITIONAL BACKGROUND MATERIALS

Archdeacon, T. (1983). *Becoming American: An Ethnic History*. Free Press. New York.

Muller, T. and Espenshade, T. (1985). *The Fourth Wave*. Urban Institute Press. Washington, D. C.

United Nations Population Fund
220 East 42nd Street
New York, New York 10017

The Futurist
Published by the World Future Society
4916 Saint Elmo Ave.
Bethesda, Maryland 20814

DEALING WITH DIVERSITY — CLASS 5
Immigration Policy in the United States of America

I. INTRODUCTION

In this class we will examine the history of immigration laws in the U.S. We will begin by examining the various waves of immigrants who came to the U.S., the reasons why they came, and their reactions after they got here. We will also listen to an interview with Marian Smith of the Immigration and Naturalization Service (INS). She will describe some of the rationale for the establishment of the early immigration laws. Our in-class guest is Susan Gzesh, a lawyer who specializes in immigration cases.

It is important when you listen to the discussion of our guests and students that you keep in mind the perspective of the immigrant as well as the various opinions and views that make up the populist philosophy that shapes the policy makers in our government.

Before you watch the videotape for this lesson:
READ: 27: "Civil Rights Issues Facing Asian Americans in the United States" in *The Meaning of Difference*, pages 315-330.

II. VIDEO INSERTS

The first video insert for this class was shot in Washington D.C. at the National Archives. The interview was conducted with Constance Potter, Director of the Microfilm Department. As you watch this interview consider the following questions:

A. What are some of the ways that a person may be able to access the records in the archives to find out about the arrival of their ancestors into the U.S.?

B. What is the basic information a person would need in order to access this information?

The second video insert in this class was also shot in Washington D.C. at the headquarters for the Immigration and Naturalization Service (INS). The interview was with Marian Smith, Chief Librarian at INS. As you watch this interview consider the following questions:

A. What were some of the earliest immigration policies developed in the U.S.? Why were they developed?

B. When did the INS come into existence, and under what part of the government was it initially?

C. List and describe some of the major immigration laws that influenced the preference for immigrants from certain countries over those of other countries.

D. What impact did our nation's immigration laws have on Asian-Americans and when were these conditions relieved?

 At this stage we suggest you watch the videotape.

III. REVIEW QUESTIONS

Now that you have completed the readings and reviewed the videotape for this class you should answer the following questions to make sure you understand the key concepts presented.

1. Briefly explain some of the reasons this nation developed its policies on immigration.

2. Review some of the major immigration laws from the 19th and 20th century that shaped the way our population looks.

3. According to Gzesh the INS has not always acted in a fair and unbiased manner. Cite at least two examples that might give credence to her assumptions.

4. The 1924 National Origins Act was a landmark decision in the history of the U.S. immigration policy. Explain how public opinion and the findings of the Dillingham Commission influenced the development of these laws.

5. In the article "Civil Rights Issues Facing Asian Americans in the 1990's," list and discuss the chronology of naturalization and immigration laws that have limited the access of Asian people coming to the U.S.A.

IV. SUGGESTED ADDITIONAL BACKGROUND MATERIALS

Fix, M. and Passel, J. (1991). *The Door Remains Open: Recent Immigration to the United States and a Preliminary Analysis of the Immigration Act of 1990.* Urban Institute Press, Washington, D.C.

Espenshade, T. et. al. (1988). *Immigration Policy in the United States: Future Prospects for the Immigration Reform and Control Act of 1986.* Urban Institute Press, Washington, D.C.

DEALING WITH DIVERSITY — CLASS 6
Race: The World's Most Dangerous Myth

I. INTRODUCTION

This class explores one of our nation's most complex and pressing problems, the concept of race. Deeply rooted in our historical past, this concept has multiple meanings for each and every one of us. The significance lies deep in our enculturation and is manifested as much in the educational curriculum as it is in the societal curriculum. The problem surrounding race is exacerbated by the multiple definitions that have been given to it as you will see in this video. To help you understand the differences between how science utilizes the concept of race as compared to the social definitions that are often used, our in-class guest is Dr. Bem Allen, a social psychologist from Western Illinois University.

Recent research on racial attitude formation among children suggests that our schools may be part of the problem. Be sure to read in detail the article by Garcia.

Before you watch the videotape for this lesson:
READ: 1: "Who is Black? One Nation's Definition" in *The Meaning of Difference*, pages 35-42.
2: "La Raza and the Melting Pot: A Comparative Look at Multiethnicity" in *The Meaning of Difference*, pages 43-51.
Ashley Montagu's "Statement on Race," reproduced below.

(a) In matters of race, the only characteristics which anthropologists can effectively use as a basis for classifications are physical and physiological.

(b) According to present knowledge there is no proof that the groups of mankind differ in their innate mental characteristics, whether in respect of intelligence or temperament. The scientific evidence indicates that the range of mental capacities in all ethnic groups is much the same.

(c) Historical and sociological studies support the view that genetic differences are not of importance in determining the social and cultural differences between different groups of *Homo sapiens*, and that the social and cultural changes in different groups have, in the main, been independent of changes in inborn constitution. Vast social changes have occurred which were not in any way connected with changes in racial type.

(d) There is no evidence that race mixture as such produces bad results from the biological point of view. The social results of race mixture whether for good or ill are to be traced to social factors.

(e) All normal human beings are capable of learning to share in a common life, to understand the nature of mutual service and reciprocity, and to respect social obligations and contracts. Such biological differences as exist between members of different ethnic groups have no relevance to problems of social and political organization, moral life and communication between human beings.

From: A. Montagu, (1972), *Statement on Race*, Oxford University Press, Oxford, England

Exercises you might like to perform before you watch the tape.

A. At the beginning of the videotape the teleclass students are asked to come up with a racial classification system. See if you can produce one of your own from the list below. Try and group people together, and then when you watch the tape compare your classifications with those the students generate.

Common descriptions of people

African	African American	American	Mongoloid
American Indian	Arab	Asian	Polynesian
Australoid	Black	Caucasian	White
Caucasoid	Chinese	Eskimo	Native-American
European	Filipino	Hawaiian	Slavic
Hebrew	Indian	Japanese	Negroid
Latino	Melanesian	Micronesian	South East Asian

B. Test your "Racism Quotient" by filling out the "Racism Quotient" questionnaire reproduced below. Some of these questions will be discussed in the videotape. There are no "answers" to the test, but you will find that by filling it out you will learn something about your own beliefs and feelings about race. (However, you can receive a "score" and explanation if you send your answers to: *"RQ TEST, c/o The Village Voice, VPV 1001, 36 Cooper Square, New York, NY 10003,* including a stamped self-addressed envelope.)
(Test reproduced courtesy of Carol Taylor, RN)

1. With what racial origin or background do you identify yourself?
   (Check as many as apply.)

   A. Native American   E. East Indian
   B. Caucasian   F. Asian
   C. Black   G. Aborigine
   D. Hispanic   H. Other

2. At a social gathering of 30-40 people, you enter a room where you appear to be the only member of your ethnic group. You would most likely:

   A. Leave the room in search of members of your own ethnic group
   B. Stand around and hope someone would talk with you
   C. Open a conversation with whomever looks interesting
   D. Feel bored or uncomfortable and wish you hadn't come

3. A close friend calls to tell you her son/daughter is engaged to marry a person of another race. You would most likely feel:

   A. Appalled and warn her of the possible consequences
   B. Delighted that your friend's child has found someone to share her/his life
   C. Surprised but somewhat skeptical as to the wisdom of such a marriage
   D. Sad because of all of the trouble they are probably going to encounter

4. A person of a different ethnic background is elected to a high office instead of a candidate of your ethnicity. You would feel:

   A. No special feelings if he/she seemed to be the best person for the job
   B. Somewhat threatened now that more of "them" are taking over
   C. Upset because you voted for someone else you really believed in
   D. Not too concerned, but suspect that sooner or later he/she/they will do something disgraceful

5. A museum will soon open in your neighborhood with displays of culture far removed ethnically and geographically from yours. You would most likely:

   A. Probably not visit it because you couldn't identify with it
   B. Consider it an interesting place to visit because it is different
   C. Write your congressperson protesting that the museum should reflect your neighborhood's culture
   D. Organize a children's group and take it for a visit

6. You belong to a club that has a few minority members, one of whom (as well as a majority member) is running for president. The majority member shares your racial background. Before voting, you would most likely:

   A. Assume that the majority member is the best person for the job
   B. Thoroughly investigate the majority member's background
   C. Encourage other members of your race to vote for the majority member
   D. Investigate the credentials and desirability of both candidates

7. You are told by a recognized authority that your 12 year old would fare better educationally if she/he were bused to a more distant location where she/he would be in the extreme minority. Your reaction would be to:

   A. Immediately remove your child and have her/him bused to the new location
   B. Discuss the possibility with your child and investigate the new location together before making a decision
   C. Let your child stay where she/he is. It will be emotionally more comfortable for the child
   D. Investigate the merits of the new location yourself before making up your mind

8. A couple of your own race in your neighborhood decides to adopt a child of a different race. Your feelings are that:

   A. The child will fare well depending upon how nurturing and loving the parents are
   B. The child will probably suffer because she/he is "different" from the other children in the neighborhood
   C. The couple should move to a mixed neighborhood where the "different" child won't stand out
   D. If the couple wants to take that kind of chance, you're glad the child has found a home

9. You need to process a complicated business transaction at a bank. There are three or four available managers, all of different racial backgrounds. You will probably:

   A. Choose one of your own racial background. She/he will probably understand your needs better
   B. Choose the one closest to you. After all, they're all trained to do the same thing
   C. Ask the receptionist which banker might best serve your particular needs
   D. Pick the banker who is the best groomed and has the most welcoming smile

10. The newspaper headlines often focus on articles concerning international and/or foreign politics about unreal struggles for freedom, human rights for Jews in Russia, apartheid in South Africa, or the plight of half-Vietnamese children. Your attitude is:

    A. The United states should steer clear whenever possible of such controversy. These are really not our problems.
    B. People all over the world have a right to support and help in their fight for liberation and human rights, regardless of how much it upsets the status quo
    C. Many of these countries were peaceful until their minorities or dissidents began to relocate, protest, or riot
    D. Those in power should gradually make changes to support and accommodate minorities or the oppressed

11. You are invited to a racially mixed picnic. Everyone has been asked to bring a sample of their own ethnic cuisine. Having no dietary restrictions, you would most probably:

    A. Bring something that is commonly accepted among all ethnic groups
    B. Eat only what you have brought: you are a little suspicious of what ingredients are in some of the other dishes
    C. Be curious and willing to sample a little of what everyone else has brought
    D. Question what is in each dish before deciding whether you will sample it.

12. You are a teacher in a junior high school and the administration has suggested a course in "black English" be introduced into the curriculum. Your attitude is:

    A. Since black students do speak differently, it might be easier to teach them in their own jargon
    B. Black students would welcome the change and feel a lot more comfortable
    C. The majority culture in which most black students will ultimately work does not communicate in "black English," so such as course would be doing black students a disservice
    D. Most black students are never going to master the King's English, so at least they will be educated in their own way of speaking

13. Recently, Martin Luther King's birthday was made into a national holiday. Previously, only the birthdays of prominent white Americans were celebrated. Your attitude about this is:

A. Blacks will pursue any opportunity to be equal with whites, deserved or not
B. If we turned every martyred hero's birthday into a holiday, pretty soon there wouldn't be any work days
C. Martin Luther King's nonviolent protest against appalling social conditions was deserving of such recognition
D. Considering what blacks have invested in this country, it's time they had their own holiday

14. During World War II, atomic bombs were dropped on Japan but not on the other two Axis nations (Germany and Italy). Our last two wars were with Koreans and Vietnamese. Which statement below comes closest to your reaction to the above statement:

A. I notice that our last three wars did the most damage to non-Caucasians
B. The Japanese are sneaky and pulled a sneak attack on us. We were justified in dropping the A-bomb on them
C. The Koreans and Vietnamese were themselves divided, so we were fighting with them as well as against them
D. Any means we employed to end any war was justifiable

15. A Hispanic youngster stopped by the police late at night appeared to make a threatening gesture and was critically shot by the police. No weapon was found on him. Your reaction to this is:

A. What did he expect, being out on the streets at that late hour of night?
B. The police had a right to defend themselves against a threatening gesture. They often have to make quick decisions
C. Hispanics are noted for their quick tempers, so it's understandable that the police reacted as they did
D. Did the police exhaust all avenues of investigation and warning before pulling the trigger?

16. At your place of business, the head of personnel has a choice of hiring an eminently qualified black and an equally qualified white for a policy-making (hiring/firing) position. You are asked by secret ballot after reading their qualifications to make your choice. You feel:

A. I would choose one of my own racial group. He would understand my problems better and I'd be more likely to keep my job
B. If the person picked is not of my race, they will undoubtedly begin to hire members of their own group and try taking over
C. I would choose the black person because chances are she/he has worked harder and is more qualified for the position and will be more fair in dealing with others different from her/himself
D. If they are equally qualified, my choice will be based on each one's knowledge of the inner workings of the company and how well she/he communicates and deals with people

17. You have been hospitalized for a somewhat serious illness and confined for at least a week in a semi-private room. Your roommate is of a different race. Your reaction is:

   A. Grin and bear it; it's only going to be for a week
   B. If you're not too ill, be glad to have someone to talk with occasionally
   C. Go out of your way to be pleasant; you don't want your roommate thinking you have racial hang-ups
   D. You're not familiar with people of other races, but if they seem friendly, you'll try to be friendly too

18. When you're out in public and see couples or lovers of obviously different racial backgrounds - i.e. black/white, Asian/Hispanic, Indian/white, your reaction is:

   A. If these two people want to be together, it doesn't make any difference to me; it's their problem
   B. It doesn't bother me as long as it doesn't happen in my family
   C. As long as neither of them is from Mars I say, "Hooray for lovers!"
   D. I don't believe in mixing the races

19. Assuming that there is a grave national and worldwide problem of racism, which of the following best expresses how you feel about it?

   A. Leave it alone; it will work itself out naturally
   B. Start teaching your children early on about the commonality of human beings and the human experience
   C. Keep the races separated and you won't have the problem
   D. I don't believe we live in a racially prejudiced society

20. If you were not of the racial or ethnic origin you believe yourself to be, which of the following would you choose to be? (Check as many as apply.)

   A. The one I am   F. East Indian
   B. Native American   G. Asian
   C. Caucasian   H. Aborigine
   D. Black   I. Other
   E. Hispanic   J. It doesn't matter

II. VIDEO INSERTS

The video interview for this class was with Dr. Jerry Hirsch, a distinguished professor in psychology and genetics at the University of Illinois Champaign-Urbana. Dr. Hirsch has been conducting research on race for over 30 years and is considered one of our nation's leading experts in this field. As you watch this interview consider the following questions:

A. What kind of experimentation has Dr. Hirsch been involved in to try and determine if genetic races can be evolved?

B. Who are the "charlatans" that Dr. Hirsch discusses in this interview?

C. Why does Dr. Hirsch consider race to be one of man's most dangerous myths?

III. GRAPHICS

 At this stage we suggest you watch the videotape. The graphics you will see on the screen are reproduced below to save you the trouble of copying them down. You might like to add your own comments as you watch the tape.

Montagu's Four Major Human Races

■ Negroid
■ Archaic White or Australoid
■ Caucasoid or White
■ Mongoloid

Oliver's Seven Major Races

■ Early Mongoloid
■ Late Mongoloid
■ Negro
■ Bushman
■ Australian
■ Pygmy Negroid
■ White

18th Century European Races

■ Teutonic
■ Alpine
■ Mediterranean

Puerto Rican Racial Classifications

- Blanco (white)
- Preito (dark skinned)
- Trigueno (tan)

Geographic Races

- African
- American Indian
- Asian
- Australian
- European
- Indian
- Melanesian
- Micronesian
- Polynesian

Major Geographical Races

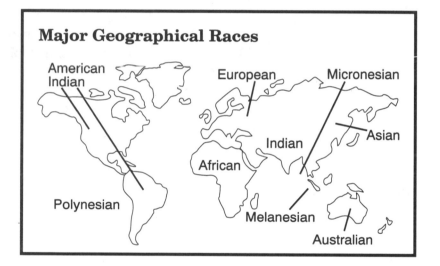

Classifications in New Spain

Spaniard & Indian >>> Mestizo
Mestizo & Spanish Woman >>> Castizo
Spaniard & Castizo Woman >>> Spaniard
Negro & Spanish Woman >>> Mulatto
Spaniard & Mulatto Woman >>> Morisco
Spaniard & Morisco Woman >>> Albino

**Some Genetically Determined
Race Differences**

- ABO blood-group system
- RH blood-group factor
- MNS blood-group system
- Lactose deficiency
- Missing third molar teeth
- Wristbone fusions
- Color blindness
- Sickle cell gene

IV. REVIEW QUESTIONS

Now that you have completed the readings and viewed the videotape for this class you should answer the following questions to make sure you understand the key concepts presented.

1. Why is race considered an invalid paradigm?

2. What is the difference between the social and biological use of the term 'race'?

3. If race is an invalid paradigm, why does it persist in our society in the manner that it does?

4. Explain why the research and dogma of such individuals as Jensen, Shockley, and others does not enjoy widespread support in the scientific community.

5. According to the article "Who is Black?" explain why it has been so difficult for this nation to give up the "One Drop Rule" as it applies to the designation of race for people of African descent.

6. Discuss the differences between the racial classification systems of Anglo America and Latin America as described in the article "La Raza and the Melting Pot."

V. SUGGESTED ADDITIONAL BACKGROUND MATERIALS

Taylor, C. and Saunders, M. P. *Racism Quotient Questionnaire*. In the Village Voice, February 11, 1992. "Are you a Racist?" by Peter Noel.

Montagu, A. (1972). Statement on Race. In A. Montagu's, *Statement On Race*. New York: Oxford University Press.

Montagu, A. (1974). *Man's Most Dangerous Myth. The Fallacy of Race*. 5th Edition. New York: Oxford University Press.

Hirsch, J. (1975). Jensenism: The Bankruptcy of "Science" Without Scholarship. In *Educational Theory*. Winter, Vol. 25, NI. 1975.

Hirsch, J. (1981). To "Unfrock the Charlatans". In *Sage Race Relations Abstracts*. Vol. 6, NZ, May 1981.

McCarthy, C. and Crichlow, W. (1993). *Race Identity and Representation in Education*, New York, Routledge.

West, C. (1994). *Race Matters*, Beacon Press.

DEALING WITH DIVERSITY — CLASS 7
Native American Cultures in the United States: Part 1

I. INTRODUCTION

This is the first of two classes on the Native American cultures in the U.S. In the first class we will examine some of the origins of Native Americans on the North American continent, as well as present some background to their current state in society. Our two in-studio guests are Mr. Paul Schranz, University Professor of Photography at Governors State University, and Mr. Jerry Lewis, a historian. Paul has over the years collected a number of pictures of commercial art featuring Native Americans. As you watch his slides, notice how they convey generally unflattering stereotypes of the Native American.

Mr. Lewis is a member of the Potawatomi tribe. He has performed considerable research on treaties signed between the U.S. government and various Native American groups. Treaty rights are becoming a considerable source of friction between Native Americans and their neighbors, and Mr. Lewis will present you with some useful background on how these treaties originated.

Be sure to focus on some of the many issues surrounding the issue of sovereignty with Native American groups in our country. For example, are Native Americans citizens of the U.S.? What rights do Non-Indians have on Native American reservations? Are there continuing disputes over treaties between our country and various Native American groups?

Before you watch the videotape for this lesson:
READ: 21: "Ten Key Supreme Court Cases" in *The Meaning of Difference*, pages 251-272.

II. GRAPHICS

At this stage we suggest you watch the videotape. The graphics you will see on the screen are reproduced below to save you the trouble of copying them down. You might like to add your own comments as you watch the tape.

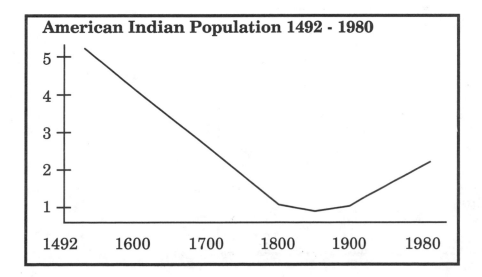
American Indian Population 1492 - 1980

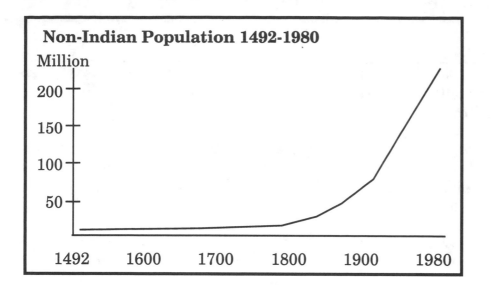

Non-Indian Population 1492-1980

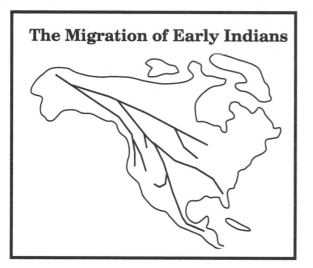

The Migration of Early Indians

Indian Population Estimates – Millions			
Date	Author	Western Hemisphere	North America
1924	Rivet	40 - 50	1.1
1924	Supper	40 - 50	2 - 3.5
1939	Krober	8.4	.9
1949	Steward	15.5	1.0
1966	Dobyns	90	9.8
1976	Ubelaker	—	2.2
1981	Thornton and Marsh-Thornton	—	7.7
1983	Dobyns	—	18.0

> *"Where today are the Pequot?*
> *Where are the Narragansett,*
> *the Mohican, the Pokanoket,*
> *and many other once powerful*
> *tribes of our people? They have*
> *vanished before the avarice and*
> *the oppression of the White Man,*
> *as snow before a summer sun."*
> **Tecumseh** (Shawnee)

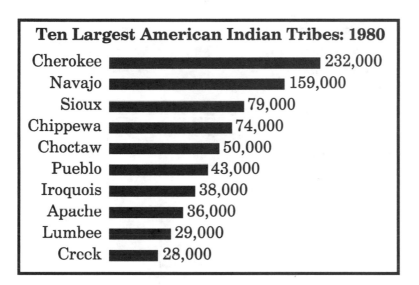

Ten Largest American Indian Tribes: 1980

Tribe	Population
Cherokee	232,000
Navajo	159,000
Sioux	79,000
Chippewa	74,000
Choctaw	50,000
Pueblo	43,000
Iroquois	38,000
Apache	36,000
Lumbee	29,000
Creek	28,000

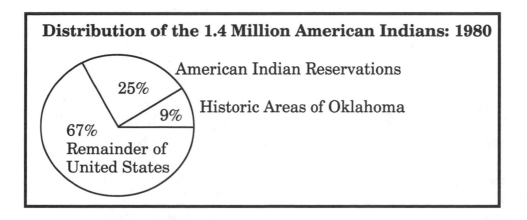

Distribution of the 1.4 Million American Indians: 1980

25% American Indian Reservations

9% Historic Areas of Oklahoma

67% Remainder of United States

The Societal Curriculum

The massive, ongoing, informal curriculum of family, peer groups, neighborhoods, churches, organizations, occupations, mass media, and other socializing forces that "educate" all of us throughout our lives.
(Carlos E. Cortes)

U.S. Constitution, Article 1

Section 2.
Representatives and direct taxes shall be apportioned among the several states . . . which shall be determined by adding to the whole number of free persons, including those bound to service for a term of years, and EXCLUDING INDIANS NOT TAXED.

U.S. Constitution, Amendment 14

Section 2.
Representatives shall be apportioned among the several states according to their respective numbers, counting the whole number of persons in each state, EXCLUDING INDIANS NOT TAXED.

**South Half or Diminished
Colville Indian Reservation**

Mr. J.M. Johnson, the superintendent of Indian affairs, located at Nespelem, handles this business for the Indians. Mr. Johnson is an agreeable man to meet, thoroughly posted, and handles these transactions for the Indians in a capable manner. He is always at the service of those seeking information concerning the lease or sale of Indian allotments. A letter addressed to him at Nespelem will receive Mr. Johnson's personal attention, I can assure you. Many of these allotments are still in the primitive state, having been alloted to Indians now deceased, or too old or infirm to work them. These allotments may be appraised by Mr. Johnson, and a valuation be put on them, and sold to the highest bidder. The allotments when advertised, are published by name and number and can be readily located on the map.

III. REVIEW QUESTIONS

Now that you have done the readings and viewed the video tape you should answer the following question to make sure you understand the key concepts.

1. According to Western historians describe the popular theory on how the various Native American groups arrived on the North American continent.

2. How does the theory you describe in question number one agree or disagree with the creation stories told by Native Americans themselves?

3. Why is the debate between researchers on the number of Native Americans at the time of contact with Columbus and the West so crucial to our understanding of what has happened to these indigenous people?

4. How do you think Native Americans might feel about seeing their tribe or other
   Native Americans depicted in the slides shown by Professor Schranz?

5. What might be some of the consequences of America's long term consumption of negative/distorted images of Native Americans?

6. What is it that we can learn from some of the past dealings with Native American peoples that Jerry Lewis describes? How can this help us understand their current state of existence in our country?

7. List some of the contributions that have been borrowed from Native Americans and are now part of the American culture.

8. Carefully read the Supreme Court case "Elk v. Wilkins" (1884) and describe the decision made by the court. Speculate what the likely consequences were for Native Americans living during that time.

VI. SUGGESTED ADDITIONAL BACKGROUND MATERIALS

Thornton, R., (1987). *American Indian Holocaust and Survival, A Population History Since 1492*. University of Oklahoma Press: Norman, Ok.

Gibson, A. M., (1980). *The American Indian: Prehistory to the Present*. D.C. Heath and Company: Lexington, Ma.

de Las Casas, Bartoleme (1974). *In Defense of the Indian*. Northern Illinois University Press. DeKalb, Ill.

de Las Casas, Bartoleme, (1953). *Tears of Indians*. Stanford, Ca.

Helps, Sir Arthur, (1970). *The Life of Las Casas*. The John Lilburne Co., Williamston, Mass.

Leustig, J. and Grossman, R. (1995). *500 Nations Miniseries*, Burbank, CA: Warner Home Video.

I. INTRODUCTION

This is the second class that has focused on the history of Native Americans in our nation. In this class we will use a case study format to examine the controversy surrounding the Dickson Mounds Museum Burial Grounds, regarding the appropriateness of displaying human remains found in ancient Native American burial grounds. In the second part of the lesson our in-studio guests are Mr. James Yellowbank, Coordinator of the Indian Treaty Rights Committee, and Roxie Grignon of TEARS (**T**o **E**nable our **A**ncestors **R**eturn to the **S**pirit world). Again the issue is treaty rights, and they present an eloquent description of the moral and legal responsibilities inherent in honoring treaties made many years ago. (Please note: After the lesson for this course was videotaped, the decision was made by Governor Edgar of Illinois to rebury the human remains at Dickson Mounds, and allow them, as you will hear James Yellowbank say, "to continue on their journey.")

II. VIDEO INSERTS

The video insert for this class presents a case study on the controversy surrounding the burial grounds at the Dickson Mounds Museum in Lewiston, Illinois, where remains of ancient Native Americans are on display. The issue is whether or not the mounds should be closed and the bones reburied. As in most controversies there are two sides. As you watch this case study consider the following questions:

A. According to Professor Conrad what are some of the scientific reasons for keeping the burial grounds open?

B. Representative Edley refers to a Pan-Indian religious movement as a rationale for the Native Americans to protest the closing of the burial grounds. What does he mean by a Pan-Indian movement?

C. What is your opinion about viewing the burial remains of any deceased cultural group?

CLASS 8

 At this stage we suggest you watch the videotape.

III. REVIEW QUESTIONS

Now that you have done the reading for this class and viewed the videotape you should answer the following questions to make sure you understand the key concepts presented in this class.

1. Discuss the controversy surrounding the Dickson Mound Burial Grounds from the perspective of both the Native Americans as well as people like Dr. Conrad and Representative Edley.

2 What is it that James Yellowbank feels that current Native Americans can teach this generation of Americans in the United States?

IV. SUGGESTED ADDITIONAL BACKGROUND MATERIALS

Smith, R. M. (1991). *Columbus Special Issue: When Worlds Collide*, Newsweek, Fall/Winter.

Graves, W. (1991). *1491 America Before Columbus*. The National Geographic Society, October 1991. Vol. 180, No. 4

Native American Grave and Burial Protection Act (Repatriation); Native American Repatriation of Cultural Patrimony Act; and Heard Museum Report: Hearing Before the Select Committee on Indian Affairs U.S. Senate, 101st Congress, Second Session, S.1021 & S.1980. May 14, 1990. Washington, D.C.

Woodhead, H., Series Editor (1996). *The American Indians*, Time-Life Books: Richmond, VA.

DEALING WITH DIVERSITY — CLASS 9
Hispanic-American Cultures in the United States of America

I. INTRODUCTION

This class concentrates on the multiple ethnic groups we classify as Hispanics. It is very important that as you learn about these groups you begin to understand the similarities as well as the differences between these diverse groups.

Our special guest for this class is Dr. Samuel Betances, Professor of Sociology, at Northeastern Illinois University in Chicago, Illinois. Dr. Betances is considered a national and international expert in the area of Hispanic and Multicultural concerns. Be sure that you understand the variety of provocative issues Betances discusses throughout this class, for example: Why is Bilingual Education so important given our changing demography? Why is it impossible to group all Hispanics as a homogeneous group? What problems exist with defining race in Puerto Rico? What changes need to happen in our colleges and universities?

 Before you watch the videotape for this lesson:
READ: 28: "Making Sense of Diversity: Recent Research on Hispanic Minorities in the United States" in *The Meaning of Difference*, pages 330-336.

II. VIDEO INSERTS

The video insert for this class is at the very beginning of the videotape. It provides a very dramatic introduction to the culture and history of Mexican Americans.

III. GRAPHICS

 At this stage we suggest you watch the videotape. The graphics you will see on the screen are reproduced below to save you the trouble of copying them down. You might like to add your own comments as you watch the tape.

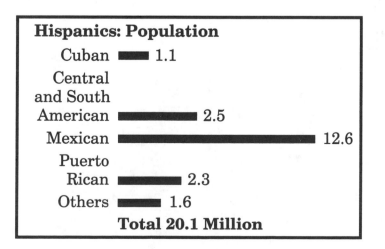

Hispanics: Population

Cuban ▬ 1.1
Central and South American ▬▬▬ 2.5
Mexican ▬▬▬▬▬▬▬▬ 12.6
Puerto Rican ▬▬ 2.3
Others ▬ 1.6
Total 20.1 Million

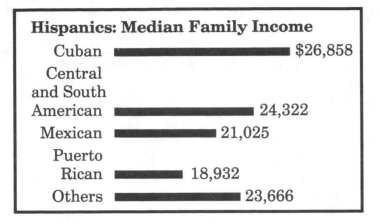

Hispanics: Median Family Income

Cuban	$26,858
Central and South American	24,322
Mexican	21,025
Puerto Rican	18,932
Others	23,666

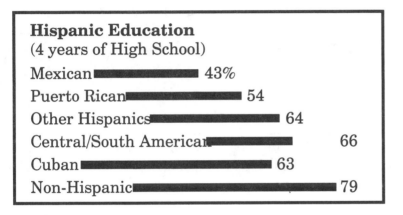

Hispanic Education
(4 years of High School)

Mexican	43%
Puerto Rican	54
Other Hispanics	64
Central/South American	66
Cuban	63
Non-Hispanic	79

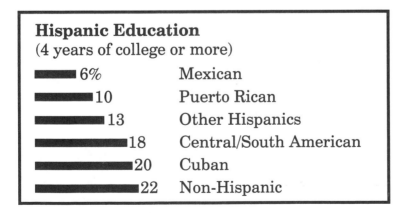

Hispanic Education
(4 years of college or more)

6%	Mexican
10	Puerto Rican
13	Other Hispanics
18	Central/South American
20	Cuban
22	Non-Hispanic

Hispanic Families: Poverty Level

	Total	Number Below Poverty	Percent Below Poverty
Mexican-American	2,805	701	25%
Puerto Rican	637	196	31%
Cuban	322	54	17%
Central and South American	630	104	17%
Other	430	88	20%
All Hispanics	4,824	1,140	24%

IV. REVIEW QUESTIONS

Now that you have completed the reading and viewed the videotape for this class you should answer the following questions to make sure you understand the key concepts presented.

1. Name at least 10 groups that are classified under the term Hispanic.

2. What group of Hispanics do not have to have a passport to enter the U.S.?

3. Why is it that some Hispanic groups have fared better economically and educationally than some others?

4. Dr. Betances argues the importance of teaching students in their mother tongue; explain why he feels this position is so important.

5. Describe how Dr. Betances would reform colleges and universities to accommodate the diversity of students in our classrooms today and in the future.

6. In the article "Making Sense of Diversity: Recent Research on Hispanic Minorities in the United States" the author argues that the *mode of incorporation* of each immigrant minority group is significant in how that group will be treated economically. What example does the author cite as evidence? Would Dr. Betances support this position?

V. SUGGESTED ADDITIONAL BACKGROUND MATERIALS

Miller, S. (1992). Caught Between Two Cultures. *Newsweek* V119 N16, pp. 32-35.

Walsh, C. (1991). *Pedagogy and the Struggle for Voice: Issues of Language, Power, and Schooling for Puerto Ricans*. Bergin & Garvey. New York.

Santiago, A. (1992). Patterns of Puerto Rican Segregation and Mobility. *Hispanic Journal of Behavioral Sciences*. V14 N1, pp. 144-157.

Sodowsky, G., Lai, E., and Plake, B. (1991). Moderating Effects of Sociocultural Variables on Acculturation Attitudes of Hispanics and Asian Americans. *Journal of Counseling and Development*. V70 N1, pp. 194-205.

Llanes, Jose, (1982). *Cuban Americans: Masters of Survival*. Cambridge, Mass., Abbott Books.

DEALING WITH DIVERSITY — CLASS 10
African-American Cultures in the U.S.A: Part 1

I. INTRODUCTION

This is the first of two classes exploring African-American culture in the United States. In Part 1, we will examine the changing statistical and demographic data of this group and how it compares to other groups in our society. As we look at these differences it is important to understand some of the root causes of these differences and explore possible solutions to these disparities. One of the possible solutions is to change our current educational curriculum. Be sure to understand the rationale behind this possible remedy and the impact that it would likely have on our schools and community. Our video insert for this class is an interview with Dr. Molefi Asante, Chairperson of the African American Studies Department at Temple University. Dr. Asante is considered one of our nation's leading proponents of the Afrocentric Movement, one of the current strategies being used to reform the curriculum of our schools.

Edward Johnson, a counselor at Joliet Junior College in Joliet, Illinois is our in-studio guest for this class. Johnson shares his years of experience to help us understand some of the reasons that African American students do not fare as well as other ethnic groups in our society. Be sure to note how various individuals in the class interpret why there are differences in the performance of African American students in our schools.

 Before you watch the videotape for this lesson:
READ: 31: "The Health of Black Folk: Disease, Class, and Ideology in Science" in *The Meaning of Difference*, pages 376-381.

II. VIDEO INSERTS

There are two video inserts in this class. The class opens with the first insert, which is taken from a Kwanza celebration held at Temple University. As you watch this video insert consider the following questions:

A. What is the significance of the clothing of most of the participants of this event?

B. The participants are singing Nkosi sikeleli-Afrika (The South African National Anthem) associated with the African National Congress, a political party in South Africa. Why do you think this song is being sung with such reverence?

In the second video insert you see an interview with Dr. Molefi Asante, Chairperson of the African-American Studies Department at Temple University, in Philadelphia, Pa. After you watch this insert consider the following questions:

A. Why does Dr. Asante think it is important for African American children to be grounded in an African-centric educational curriculum?

B. What role should the African-centric curriculum play in multicultural education?

C. A group of young African Americans, from an African-centric School called "The Academy of the Way," are shown singing a song "Malcolm X is a Friend of Mine." According to Asante's assertions, what is the likely long term impact of this type of schooling on these young people?

III. GRAPHICS

At this stage we suggest you watch the videotape. The graphics you will see on the screen are reproduced below to save you the trouble of copying them down. You might like to add your own comments as you watch the tape.

African-American Community Social Structure

Upper Class **10%**

Professionals
Managers
Working Class **35%**

Marginally Poor
Underclass **55%**

Projected U.S. Populations

Number in Millions

Group	1980	2000	2020
White	181.0	200.3	205.6
Black	26.5	36.4	44.4
Hispanic	14.6	30.3	46.6
Asian/Other	4.4	12.1	20.3
Total U.S. Population	**226.5**	**279.1**	**316.9**

Projected U.S. Populations

Percent of Total

Group	1980	2000	2020
White	79.9	71.7	64.9
Black	11.7	13.0	14.0
Hispanic	6.4	10.8	14.7
Asian/Other	2.0	4.3	6.4
Total U.S. Population	**100.0**	**100.0**	**100.0**

Family Income by Education and Race for 1984

School	White	Black	Hispanic
Under 8	$17K	$14K	$17K
8	22	15	19
9-10	24	16	19
12	30	21	26
College	35	23	30
BA/BSC	50	37	42
Graduate	54	42	45

African-American Population by Region

Northeast	5,513,222	18.8%
Midwest	5,715,940	19.0%
South	15,828,888	52.8%
West	2,828,010	9.4%
Total	**29,986,060**	**100.0%**

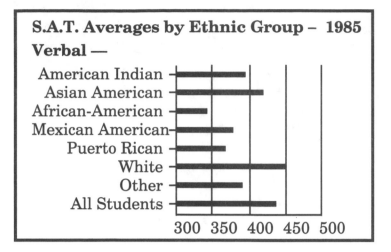

S.A.T. Averages by Ethnic Group – 1985
Verbal —

American Indian
Asian American
African-American
Mexican American
Puerto Rican
White
Other
All Students

300 350 400 450 500

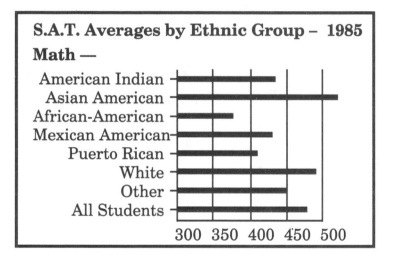

S.A.T. Averages by Ethnic Group – 1985
Math —

American Indian
Asian American
African-American
Mexican American
Puerto Rican
White
Other
All Students

300 350 400 450 500

IV. REVIEW QUESTIONS

Now that you have completed the readings and viewed the videotape you should answer the following questions to make sure you understand the key concepts presented.

1. Given the demographic data presented in this class briefly describe the current state of African Americans in the U.S.

2. There have been several theories presented in this class to try to understand the current status of African Americans in the U.S. Explain at least two of these theories and argue whether or not you think either is valid in your opinion.

3. Describe the social economic status of African Americans in this country. Why are African Americans disproportionatey represented in the low social economic status group compared to the rest of the population?

4. Discuss some of the obstacles facing Black males in our society from accessing the social mobility system.

5. In the article "The Health of Black Folk: Disease, Class, and Ideology in Science," discuss the contrast between 'the genetic model' and 'the environmental model' with regard to the health of African Americans.

V. SUGGESTED ADDITIONAL BACKGROUND MATERIALS

Asante, M. K. (1991). *Afrocentricity*. Africa World Press, Inc. Trenton, New Jersey.

Bernal, M. (1987). *Black Athena, The Afroasiatic Roots of Classical Civilization. Volume I & II*. Rutgers University Press. New Brunswick, New Jersey.

Comer, J. P. (1989). *Maggie's American Dream: The Life and Times of a Black Family*. New York: Penguin.

Fordham, S., and Ogbu, J. U. (1980). "Black Student's School Success: Coping with the 'Burden of Acting White'," *The Urban Review*, 18, 176-206.

Staples, Robert (1994). *The Black Family: Essays and Studies*. 5th Ed., Belmont, Ca: Wadsworth, Inc.

DEALING WITH DIVERSITY — CLASS 11
African American Cultures in the U.S.A: Part 2

I. INTRODUCTION

In Part 2 of the focus on African American culture in the U.S., the class centers on an interview with Dr. Jawanza Kunjufu, a prominent educator, author, and film maker. In this segment the class reacts to and discusses a variety of topics ranging from our concepts of African history and religion to the impact of African American images on the media, and the need for curricular change in our schools.

 Before you watch the videotape for this lesson:
READ: 20: "Black Sexuality: The Taboo Subject" in *The Meaning of Difference*, pages 225-229.

II. VIDEO INSERTS

This class is organized around four segments of an interview with Dr. Kunjufu. As you watch the first segment consider the following questions:

A. Why is Kunjufu critical of the depiction of African Americans in the media?

B. Why does Kunjufu argue that the description of Jesus Christ is inconsistent with the biblical description found in the New Testament?

In the second segment:

A. What can be done to help improve the academic performance of African Americans in our country?

B. What does Kunjufu attribute to why African Americans do well in some fields and not so well in other areas?

The third segment:

A. How would a multicultural curriculum change the way we see history in this country?

B. Why is Kunjufu concerned about Asian "bashing" in this country?

The fourth segment:

A. According to Kunjufu who benefits from tracking students in our educational system?

B. Why do teachers in our schools need to have more up-to-date skills to cope with the diversity of students currently in our classrooms?

 At this stage we suggest you watch the videotape.

III. REVIEW QUESTIONS

Now that you have completed the readings and viewed the videotape you should answer the following questions to make sure you understand the key concepts presented in this class:

1. Discuss some of the problems that a Eurocentric curriculum has had on the self esteem of multiple generations of African Americans in this country.

2. Kunjufu states that, "What we do most is what we do the best;" how does this help us understand why so many young African Americans are so gifted in the sports and entertainment fields?

3. Why does Cornell West in his article "Black Sexuality" claim that the demythologizing of black sexuality is so crucial for black Americans?

IV. SUGGESTED ADDITIONAL BACKGROUND MATERIALS

The following books by Dr. Jawanza Kunjufu are available through African American Images, 9204 Commercial, Suite 308, Chicago, Illinois 60617-4585

Black Communications: Breaking Down the Barriers, ISBN 0-913543-25-X

Countering the Conspiracy to Destroy Black Boys, Volume I, II, & III.

Developing Positive Self-Images and Discipline in Black Children

To Be Popular or Smart: The Black Peer Group

Kotlowitz, A. (1991). *There Are No Children Here: The Story of Two Boys Growing Up in the Other America*. New York: Doubleday.

DEALING WITH DIVERSITY — CLASS 12
Asian-American Cultures in the U.S.

I. INTRODUCTION

This is the first of two classes examining Asian American cultures in the United States. In this class we will offer an overview of some of the many groups we classify under the banner of Asian Americans. In the second class we will focus on the relationship between Korean American and African-American communities in and around Chicago, Illinois.

Our special guest for this class is Ngoan Le, Deputy Administrator, Division of Planning and Community Services, Illinois Department of Public Aid. Ms. Le came to the U.S. as a refugee from Vietnam. She also served as the Asian liaison to the Thompson administration here in the State of Illinois.

In this class be sure that you understand some of the differences as well as the similarities among the diverse groups under the umbrella we call Asian Americans. For example, what countries make up what is referred to as the "Chop Stick Cultures"? Why are Asian Americans often called the model American minorities? What are some of problems in the self identity and self esteem of first and second generation Asian Americans?

Before you watch the videotape for this lesson:
READ: 27: "Civil Rights Issues Facing Asian Americans in the 1990s" in *The Meaning of Difference*, pages 315-330.

II. GRAPHICS

At this stage we suggest you watch the videotape. The graphics you will see on the screen are reproduced below to save you the trouble of copying them down. You might like to add your own comments as you watch the tape.

Asian American Populations – 1980			
Rank	Ethnic Group	Number	Percent
	Total	3,466,421	100.0
1	Chinese	812,178	23.4
2	Filipino	781,894	22.6
3	Japanese	716,331	20.7
4	Asian Indian	387,223	11.2
5	Korean	357,393	10.3
6	Vietnamese	245,025	7.1
7	Other Asian	166,377	4.8

Asian American Populations – 1990			
Rank	**Ethnic Group**	**Number**	**Percent**
	Total	6,533,608	100.0
1	Filipino	1,405,146	21.5
2	Chinese	1,259,038	19.3
3	Vietnamese	859,638	13.2
4	Korean	814,495	12.5
5	Japanese	804,535	12.3
6	Asian Indian	684,339	10.5
7	Other Asian	706,417	10.8

Asian American Populations – 2000			
Rank	**Ethnic Group**	**Number**	**Percent**
	Total	9,850,364	100.0
1	Filipino	2,070,571	21.0
2	Chinese	1,683,537	17.1
3	Vietnamese	1,574,385	16.0
4	Korean	1,320,759	13.4
5	Asian Indian	1,006,305	10.2
6	Japanese	856,619	8.7
7	Other Asian	1,338,188	13.6

Asian Americans: Characteristics	Population 1980	Population 1990
Chinese	812,178	1,260,000
Japanese	716,331	800,000
Filipino (Non-Spanish)	781,894	1,410,000
Whites	180,502,838	191,594,000
African Americans	26,091,857	30,915,000
All Persons	226,545,805	252,293,000

Asian Americans: Characteristics – 1980

	Median Family Income	% High School Graduates
Chinese	$22,559	71.3%
Japanese	27,354	81.6%
Filipino	23,687	74.2%
Whites	21,014	69.6%
African Americans	12,627	51.2%
All Persons	19,917	66.5%

Immigrants from Vietnam, Laos, and Kampuchea, 1961-1987

Nation	1961-70	1971-80	1981-87
Vietnam	4,500	179,700	289,000
Kampuchea	1,200	8,400	96,100
Laos	100	22,600	112,000

Indochinese Refugees – 1985

State	Estimated Population
California	290,200
Texas	52,500
Washington	33,300
New York	25,500
Pennsylvania	24,300
Illinois	24,000

S.A.T. Averages by Ethnic Group – 1985
Verbal —

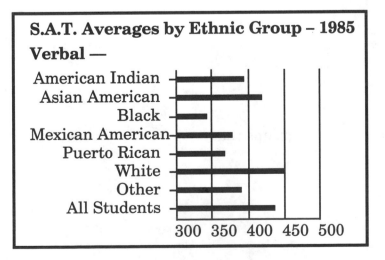

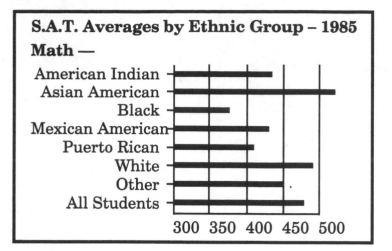

S.A.T. Averages by Ethnic Group – 1985

Math —

American Indian	
Asian American	
Black	
Mexican American	
Puerto Rican	
White	
Other	
All Students	

300 350 400 450 500

**1979 Poverty Levels
of Asian Americans**

Japanese	4.2%
Filipino	6.2%
Asian Indian	7.4%
Chinese	10.5%
Korean	13.1%
Vietnamese	35.1%
White	7.0%

III. REVIEW QUESTIONS

Now that you have completed the readings and watched the videotape for this class you should answer the following questions to make sure you understand the key concepts presented.

1. What are the ethnic groups that make up Asian Americans in this country?

2. Name the primary ethnic cultural groups that have been influenced by the Confucian philosophy.

3. How do we explain some of the economic differences between the various Asian American groups in this society?

4. Why are Asian Americans considered the "Model American Minority Group"? Why is this concept misleading?

5. Discuss why it is now more difficult for persons from South East Asia to obtain refugee status?

6. Describe some of the problems between the first and second generations of Asian Americans in this country.

7. Discuss and give reasons to support whether you agree or disagree with the seven contributing factors to Asian American equality listed in the article "Civil Rights Issues Facing Asian Americans in the 1990s."

IV. SUGGESTED ADDITIONAL READINGS

Hurh, W. M. and Kim, K. C. (1984). *Korean Immigrants in America*. Associated University Presses, Inc. Cranbury, NJ.

Melendy, H. B. (1977). *Asians in America: Filipinos, Koreans, and East Indians*. Twayne Publishers: Boston.

Nahm, A. (1988). *Korea: Tradition and Transformation of the Korean People*. Holly International Press. Elizabeth, N.J.

Takaki, R. (1989). *Strangers From A Different Shore: A History of Asian Americans*. Boston: Little, Brown and Company.

DEALING WITH DIVERSITY — CLASS 13
Korean Americans in Chicago

I. INTRODUCTION

This is the second class of looking at Asian Americans in the U.S. In this class we will focus on the Korean American community that resides in and around the city of Chicago. We will especially examine the relationship between the Korean American business community and the African American communities it serves.

The tensions between Korean Americans and African Americans discussed in this lesson dramatically exploded into violence a few weeks later in South Central Los Angeles, California in the wake of the Rodney King decision. In the light of this violence, the need to understand the underlying perspectives of both groups is ever more important. In the second part of this class we will examine a strategy to help heal the differences between the Korean American and African American communities through the common religious experience that some of their groups share.

 Before you watch the videotape for this lesson:
READ: 3: "Asian American Panethnicity" in *The Meaning of Difference*, pages 51-61.

II. VIDEO INSERTS

There are two video inserts for this class which provide a case study for the Korean American community in the Chicago area. The first video insert provides a historical and social background. In the second insert, insights into the relationships between the Korean merchants and the African American community that patronizes their businesses are presented. As you watch these video inserts consider the following questions:

A. Discuss some of the "Push-Pull" factors that influenced the decision factors for Koreans to migrate to this country.

B. What are some of the strong cultural values that still dominate the Korean community in this country?

C. How do these strong cultural values conflict with the ideas of the young American-born Koreans?

D. What are some of the identity problems faced by the Korean American community?

E. From the perspective of the Korean merchants what are some of the problems that led to the dispute between their businesses and the African American community?

F. What are some of the solutions proposed by the Korean Merchant Association to help the situation with the African-American community.

G. Describe some of the differences between the Korean American and the African American communities in the Chicagoland area.

At this stage we suggest you watch the videotape.

III. REVIEW QUESTIONS

Now that you have completed the readings and viewed the videotape for this class you should answer the following questions to make sure you understand the key concepts presented.

1. Discuss the early history of Koreans in the U.S. and describe what impact this has on contemporary issues in this country?

2. Describe some of the many problems facing Koreans as they learn to acculturate to this nation's culture.

3. Write a brief summary about some of the dissonance that has taken place between the African American and Korean American communities.

4. What are some of the successful methods that the Korean American and African American communities have established to help their current conditions?

5. Discuss in your opinion why the two Methodist churches were able to ease the conflict between the two communities.

6. In Yen Le Espirtu's article what are the factors that led the many different Asian groups in our nation to ban together in an Asian American Panethnicity?

IV. SUGGESTED ADDITIONAL READINGS

Hurh, W.M. and Kim, K.C. (1989). The 'success' image of Asian Americans: its validity, and its practical and theoretical implications. *Ethnic and Racial Studies*, Vol. 12, pp. 512-538.

Light, I. and Bonacich, E. (1988). *Immigrant Entrepreneurs: Koreans in Los Angeles, 1965-1982*. University of California Press. Berkeley.

DEALING WITH DIVERSITY — CLASS 14
European American Cultures in the U.S.

I. INTRODUCTION

The devastating ethnic strife which broke out on the disintegration of Yugoslavia brings home the realization that ethnicity can be just as powerful as race in setting people apart from people. In this class we will sample the diversity between some of the many European ethnic groups that reside in the U.S. We will look at some statistical and demographic information and discuss the changes and the stability of these groups in the U.S. mosaic.

Our special guests for this class are Dr. Dominic Candeloro, historian and administrator at Governors State University, and David Roth, Director, Institute for American Pluralism, American Jewish Committee. Dr. Candeloro is of Italian heritage and discusses some of the background culture of the Italian tradition in this country. Be sure you understand the obligations and reciprocity that mark the characteristics of the Italian American family. Is this extended family concept fading with the pressures of the new workplace in the American experience? What other changes are occurring to the traditional family values associated with Italian Americans?

When we examine the composition of the neighborhoods that make up large urban cities like Chicago, what are the forces that lead to the ethnic pattern that we currently see? Why do the neighborhoods continue to resist change? What are the benefits that we derive from the structure and function of an ethnic neighborhood? How and why do neighborhoods change?

Before you watch the videotape for this lesson:
READ: 23: "English in a Multicultural America" in *The Meaning of Difference*, pages 286-303.
24: "Whiteness as an 'Unmarked' Cultural Category" in *The Meaning of Difference*, pages 62-68.

II. GRAPHICS

At this stage we suggest you watch the videotape. The graphics you will see on the screen are reproduced below to save you the trouble of copying them down. You might like to add your own comments as you watch the tape.

Ethnic Population of 13 Colonies – 1790		
Country	**Number**	**Percentage**
English & Welsh	2,606,000	82.1%
Scottish	222,000	7.0%
German	176,000	5.6%
Dutch	79,000	2.5%
Irish	62,000	1.9%
French	18,000	0.6%
All other Europeans	11,000	0.3%

Ethnic Population of 13 Colonies – 1790
Total European population 3,172,000
Total African population 757,000

Origin of Immigrants
1820 - 1978
74.4% of immigrants were from Europe
76.0% of current population is of European origin
1981 - 1987
11.0% of immigrants were of European origin

European Immigrants to the U.S. 1981-1987

United Kingdom	99,000
Poland	52,000
Germany	49,000
Soviet Union	45,000
Portugal	29,000
Romania	26,000
Italy	24,000

III. REVIEW QUESTIONS

Now that you have completed the readings and viewed the videotape for this class you should answer the following questions to make sure you understand the key concepts presented.

1. Explain why patterns of ethnic aggregation still exist in the neighborhoods of large cities like Chicago.

2. Discuss whether the assumptions about the new development of Chicago suburbs are socioeconomically based or whether they still conform to ethnic aggregations?

3. Describe some of the images others have about Italian Americans and whether or not they are accurate.

4. What are some of the functions that neighborhoods provide for the people who live in them?

5. What was the reaction of the old immigrants at the turn of the 20th century to the new immigrants entering this country?

6. Discuss why David Roth states that using an efficiency model for dealing with diversity is impractical and prone to failure?

7. What are some of the reasons that neighborhoods change over time?

8. According to the article "English In A Multicultural America," why can't English be considered our national language?

9. List and discuss at least three different ways "whiteness" can be described in the article written by Ruth Frankenberg.

IV. SUGGESTED ADDITIONAL BACKGROUND MATERIALS

Buenker, J.D. and Ratner, L. A. eds. (1992). *Multiculturalism in the United States,*
A Comparative Guide to Acculturation and Ethnicity, Greenwood Press, New York.

Only in America. (1992). *Fortune*. V124 N13 p.183 (Dec. 2)

Not for Whites Only. (1991). *Time*. V138 N15 p.33 (Oct. 14)

DEALING WITH DIVERSITY — CLASS 15
Social Class Issues in the U.S.

I. INTRODUCTION

In this class we will look at the impact of social economics on the lives of families and individuals in the U.S. We will also focus on the plight of the homeless and what if anything can be done about this growing problem.

In the first part of the class we will examine some demographic data that illustrate the income of families by ethnic group. As you study these data, determine what are some of the factors that explain the differences in income between these groups. Why is the number of people living under the poverty level increasing? What areas of this country have the highest and lowest levels of poverty?

It is estimated that on any given night in this country between 1.5 and 3 million people are homeless, living on the streets of this nation. Why haven't we as a nation done more to remedy this tragic situation? How is it possible that in our nation's capital we have thousands of homeless people living on the streets?

In this class we will also examine the impact of social class on the plight of young people in our country. Be sure you understand how our country compares with other nations in the following areas: infant mortality, mortality rate for children under 5, and children poverty rate.

 Before you watch the videotape for this lesson:
READ: 25: "The Wage Gap: Myths and Facts" in *The Meaning of Difference*, pages 304-308.
26: "The Racial Income Gap" in *The Meaning of Difference*, pages 308-315.

II. VIDEO INSERTS

The video insert for this class is one of the most powerful in the "Dealing With Diversity" series. It presents a collage of interviews and actual visuals of homeless people in our nation's capital and in England. As you watch this insert consider the following questions.

A. What is the reaction of pedestrians as they walk past the homeless people in the video insert? Would you be likely to react the same way?

B. Listen closely to the Janice Grady interview; how does she describe what it feels like to be homeless and living on the streets?

C. According to Mike Meehan from the Center for Creative Non-Violence (CCNV) who is most likely to become homeless in the U.S.?

D. During what months did the majority of the homeless people whose ashes were at CCNV die?

III. GRAPHICS

 At this stage we suggest you watch the videotape. The graphics you will see on the screen are reproduced below to save you the trouble of copying them down. You might like to add your own comments as you watch the tape.

Family Income		
All Families	**1975**	**1989**
Number of Families	**56,245,000**	**66,090,000**
Under $10,000	9.4%	9.9%
10,000 - 24,999	27.8%	24.8%
25,000 - 49,000	41.7%	36.2%
50,000 - 74,999	15.1%	17.7%
Over $75,000	5.8%	11.3%
Median Income	**$31,620**	**$34,213**

Family Income		
Euro-Americans	**1975**	**1989**
Number of Families	**49,873,000**	**58,590,000**
Under $10,000	7.9%	7.7%
10,000-24,999	26.8%	23.9%
25,000-49,999	43.0%	37.5%
50,000-74,999	16.0%	18.7%
Over $75,000	6.3%	12.2%
Median Income	**$32,885**	**$35,975**

Family Income		
Afro-Americans	**1975**	**1989**
Number of Families	**5,586,000**	**7,470,000**
Under $10,000	23.5%	25.9%
10,000-24,999	37.3%	32.1%
25,000-49,999	36.0%	28.1%
50,000-74,999	7.1%	10.2%
Over $75,000	1.2%	3.6%
Median Income	**$20,234**	**$20,209**

Family Income		
Hispanics	**1975**	**1989**
Number of Families	**2,499,000**	**4,840,000**
Under $10,000	18.3%	18.6%
10,000-24,999	39.3%	34.0%
25,000-49,999	34.3%	32.7%
50,000-74,999	6.4%	10.2%
Over $75,000	1.7%	4.5%
Median Income	**$22,013**	**$23,446**

Poverty Line

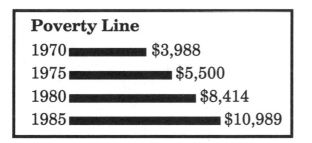

1970	$3,988
1975	$5,500
1980	$8,414
1985	$10,989

Poverty in the U.S.

Millions

1980	**1989**	**1990**
29.3	31.5	33.6

Poverty by State
Highest

Mississippi	25.7%
Louisiana	23.6%
District of Columbia	21.1%
Illinois	13.7%
Delaware	6.9%
New Hampshire	6.3%
Connecticut	6.0%

Lowest

Mortality Rate: 1989 Infants

Rank	Nation	Rate	Rank	Nation	Rate
1	Japan	4	19	Belgium	10
2	Finland	6	19	Israel	10
2	Sweden	6	19	Italy	10
4	Canada	7	19	New Zealand	10
4	Hong Kong	7	19	United States	10
4	Netherlands	7	27	Portugal	13
4	Switzerland	7	28	Bulgaria	14
8	Australia	8		Trinidad	
8	Austria	8	29	and Tobago	15
8	Denmark	8	30	Hungary	16
8	Singapore	8	30	Jamaica	16
8	United Kingdom	8	30	Poland	16
8	West Germany	8	33	Kuwait	17
17	Ireland	9	34	Costa Rica	18
17	Spain	9			

Mortality Rate: 1989
Children Younger than Five

Rank	Nation	Rate	Rank	Nation	Rate
1	Japan	6	19	Belgium	12
2	Finland	7	19	Greece	12
2	Sweden	7	19	Israel	12
4	Hong Kong	8	19	New Zealand	12
4	Netherlands	8	19	Singapore	12
6	Austria	9	19	United States	12
6	Canada	9	25	Czechoslovakia	13
6	East Germany	9	26	Cuba	14
6	France	9	27	Portugal	16
6	Switzerland	9	28	Bulgaria	17
11	Austria	10	28	Hungary	17
11	Denmark	10	30	Poland	18
11	Norway	10	30	Trinidad and Tobago	18
11	Spain	10	32	Kuwait	20
11	United Kingdom	10	33	Jamaica	21
11	West Germany	10	34	Costa Rica	22
17	Ireland	11			
17	Italy	11			

Children in Poverty

Country	Poverty Line	Below 75% of Line
Switzerland	5.1%	2.0%
Norway	7.6%	2.7%
West Germany	8.2%	2.5%
Canada	9.6%	4.4%
United Kingdom	10.7%	3.8%
Australia	16.9%	7.3%
United States	17.1%	9.8%

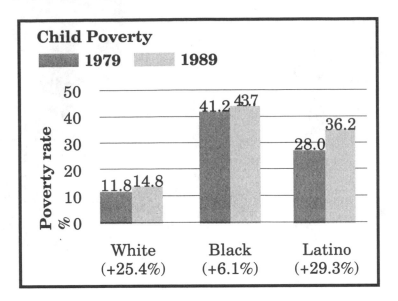

Child Poverty

■ 1979   ▨ 1989

Poverty rate %

	White (+25.4%)	Black (+6.1%)	Latino (+29.3%)
1979	11.8	41.2	28.0
1989	14.8	43.7	36.2

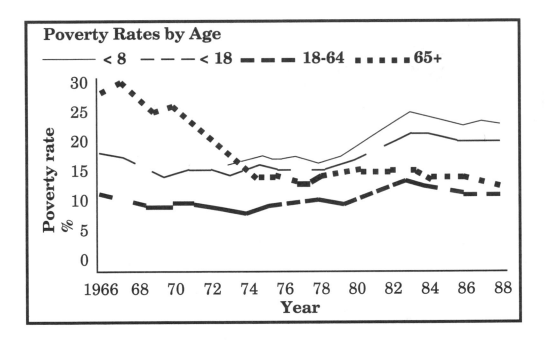

Poverty Rates by Age

——— < 8   — — — < 18   ▬ ▬ 18-64   ••••• 65+

Poverty rate %

Year

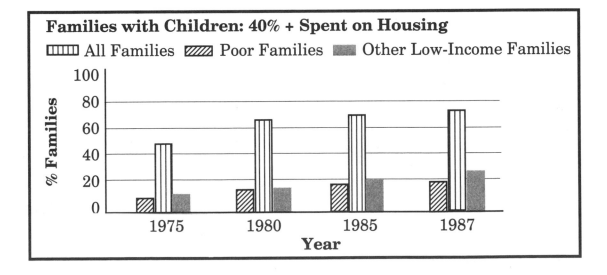

Families with Children: 40% + Spent on Housing

▥ All Families   ▨ Poor Families   ▦ Other Low-Income Families

% Families

Year

IV. REVIEW QUESTIONS

Now that you have completed the reading and viewed the videotape for this class you should answer the following questions to make sure you understand the key concepts presented.

1. Given the statistical data on family income for all groups what can we say about the incomes at the top and bottom of the income continuum?

2. Explain what the poverty line is and what groups in U.S. society are most affected by it?

3. What is the relationship between our economic system and the problems of homelessness in our nation?

4. While it is obvious that the U.S. is one of the most powerful nations in the world in some rather surprising areas we do not fare as well as we might imagine. Discuss how this rather mediocre performance could be possible.

5. According to the information presented in the article "The Wage Gap" what is the cause of this gap?

6. In the article "The Racial Income Gap" why can it be argued that educational attainment alone is not enough for blacks to close the income gap between themselves and whites?

CLASS 15

V. SUGGESTED ADDITIONAL BACKGROUND MATERIALS

Alker, J. eds. (1992). *Safety Network, The Newsletter of the National Coalition for the Homeless*.

Burt, M. and Cohen, B. (1989). *America's Homeless: Numbers, Characteristics, and Programs That Serve Them*. Urban Institute Press. Washington, D.C.

Community for Creative Non-Violence. CCNV Fact Sheet
425 2nd Street, NW, Washington, D.C. 20009

National Coalition for The Homeless
1621 Connecticut Avenue, NW
Washington, D.C. 20009

DEALING WITH DIVERSITY — CLASS 16
Age Issues in the U.S.A: Senior Citizens

I. INTRODUCTION

This is the first of two classes dealing with the continuum of age in the U.S. In this class we will focus on what life is like for our senior citizens. In the second class we will examine the often volatile period we call adolescence and the impact that gangs are having on young people in our schools and community.

One of the fastest growing segments in our society is that of adults over the age of 55. Given the fact that Americans are living longer the problems of healthcare, income, housing, and dignity are becoming a daily challenge to millions in this country.

The challenge we will have to face is not only that of government but also that of family. How will we cope with the devastation of Alzheimer disease and other maladies? When do we make the decision to place our loved ones into nursing homes? What alternatives are there to residential nursing homes?

Our special guest for this class is Kathryn Anderson, who is an active member of the Gray Panthers chapter in Chicago, Illinois. Anderson is a dynamic member of her community and is actively involved in a variety of civic issues. Be sure that you understand the importance of intergenerational contact that Anderson discusses.

II. VIDEO INSERT

The video insert for this class focuses on an Adult Day Care Center. As you watch this video insert consider the following questions:

A. What advantages does the adult daycare alternative have over the traditional nursing home facility?

B. In your opinion how did the people appear in this video insert? Did they appear to be happy and content or just going through the paces?

III. GRAPHICS

 At this stage we suggest you watch the videotape. The graphics you will see on the screen are reproduced below to save you the trouble of copying them down. You might like to add your own comments as you watch the tape.

Population by Age: Percents of Total Population

Year	Under 5	5-13	14-17	65-74	75 Plus
1960	11.3	18.2	6.2	6.1	3.1
1970	8.4	17.9	7.8	6.1	3.7
1980	7.2	13.7	7.1	6.9	4.4
1985	7.5	12.6	6.2	7.1	4.9
1989	7.6	12.8	5.4	7.3	5.1

Population by Age: Percents of Males

Year	Under 5	5-13	14-17	65-74	75 Plus
1960	11.6	18.8	6.4	5.7	2.7
1970	8.7	18.6	8.1	5.4	2.9
1980	7.6	14.3	7.4	6.1	3.2
1985	7.9	13.2	6.5	6.4	3.5
1989	7.9	13.4	5.7	6.7	3.7

Population by Age: Percents of Females

Year	Under 5	5-13	14-17	65-74	75 Plus
1960	10.9	17.7	6.1	6.5	3.5
1970	8.0	17.2	7.5	6.7	4.5
1980	6.9	13.0	6.8	7.6	5.5
1985	7.2	12.0	5.9	7.8	6.1
1989	7.2	12.2	5.2	7.9	6.5

Living Arrangements by Age: Total Population
Percent Living:

	Alone	with Spouse	with Other Rels.	with Non-Rels.
65-74	24.1	63.7	10.2	2.0
75 plus	40.5	38.5	17.8	3.1

Living Arrangements by Age: Males
Percent Living:

	Alone	with Spouse	with Other Rels.	with Non-Rels.
65-74	12.3	79.7	5.6	2.5
75 plus	21.8	65.9	9.6	2.7

Living Arrangements by Age: Females
Percent Living:

	Alone	with Spouse	with Other Rels.	with Non-Rels.
65-74	33.5	51.0	13.9	1.6
75 plus	51.5	22.5	22.6	3.4

Expenditures of the Elderly

	65-74	75 Plus	Total Population
Post Tax Income	$19,683	$12,885	$26,149
Food	3,013	1,939	3,748
Housing	6,176	4,682	8,079
Clothing & Services	977	451	1,489
Transportation	1,849	667	5,093
Health Care	2,005	2,230	1,298

Expenditures of the Elderly: Percent of Post Tax Income

	65-74	75 Plus	Total Population
Food	15.3%	15.0%	14.3%
Housing	31.4%	36.3%	30.9%
Clothing & Services	5.0%	3.5%	5.7%
Transportation	19.2%	13.7%	19.4%
Health Care	9.7%	17.3%	4.9%

Income Levels of Elderly by Households (Percent)

	Householder 65 Years Plus	Total Population
Under $5,000	7.1	5.3
5,000 - 9,999	23.6	10.3
10,000 - 14,999	17.1	9.7
15,000 - 24,999	22.0	17.9
25,000 - 34,999	12.2	15.9
35,000 - 49,999	6.6	17.3
50,000 - 74,999	5.6	14.5
75,000 Plus	3.9	9.0

World Population by Age Group – 1990

	Under 5	5-14	15-64	65 Plus
World Total	11.8	20.5	61.7	6.0
Africa	17.6	26.9	52.4	2.9
North America	7.3	14.2	66.0	12.5
Latin America	12.7	23.4	59.3	4.6
East Asia	9.3	16.5	68.0	6.2
South Asia	14.1	24.0	58.4	3.5
Europe	6.3	13.2	66.0	13.6

World Population by Age Group (Projected) – 2000

	Under 5	5-14	15-64	65 Plus
World Total	10.9	20.1	62.3	5.7
Africa	16.8	26.9	53.2	3.0
North America	6.3	13.8	66.9	13.0
Latin America	10.9	21.1	62.7	5.3
East Asia	8.6	17.0	68.7	7.6
South Asia	12.3	22.7	61.0	4.1
Europe	5.9	12.2	66.3	15.6

IV. REVIEW QUESTIONS

Now that you have completed the reading and viewed the videotape from this class you should answer the following questions to make sure you understand the key concepts presented.

1. Demographically what is happening to the various age groups in the U.S. society, especially the age group over 60?

2. What are the global age demographic trends?

3. Describe some of the most pressing problems facing senior citizens in our society.

4. Kathryn Anderson demonstrates the value, knowledge, and wisdom that senior citizens have to share with us. Discuss why we as a society do not seem to value this important resource in our culture.

5. Discuss some of the problems associated with the health care of patients in nursing homes.

6. What solutions did Anderson offer for solving the problems of senior citizens in this country?

V. SUGGESTED ADDITIONAL READINGS AND MATERIALS

Butterworth, K. (1990). *The Story of a Nursing Home Refugee.* World Earth Review. Sausalito, California.

Weiner, A. (1991). A Community-based Educational Model for Identification and Prevention of Elder Abuse. *Journal of Gerontological Social Work.* V16 N3-4 pp.107-120.

Zelman, W., Elston, J., and Weissert, W. (1991). Financial Aspects of Adult Day Care: National Survey Results. *Health Care Financing Review.* V12 N3 pp.27-37.

1989 Special Report: On Family, Whittle Communications, 505 Market Street, Knoxville, TN 37902

DEALING WITH DIVERSITY — CLASS 17
Age Issues in the U.S: Youth Culture

I. INTRODUCTION

In this second class on age issues the focus will be centered on youth culture in the U.S. We will take a introspective look at gang culture through the eyes of a police officer who is assigned to work with the gangs in Joliet Illinois public schools.

 Before you watch the videotape for this lesson:
READ: 9: "The Undeserving Poor" in *The Meaning of Difference*, pages 104-120.

II. VIDEO INSERTS

The video insert in this class contains an interview with Olivia Golden, Assistant Director of the Children's Defense Fund, headquartered in Washington, D. C. As you watch this interview consider the following questions:

A. According to Ms. Golden what is the current plight of children in America?

B. What is it that Ms. Golden says can be done to assist our communities and to improve conditions for our children?

III. GRAPHICS

 At this stage we suggest you watch the videotape. The graphics you will see on the screen are reproduced below to save you the trouble of copying them down. You might like to add your own comments as you watch the tape.

> **Joliet, Illinois**
>
> Population: 80,000
> Gang-related shootings:
>   1987 -   89
>   1988 - 107
>   1989 - 136
>   1990 - 185
>   1991 - 128

Prisons and Gangs

High School Drop-out Rate

Males	Inmates	Overall
European-Americans	71.5%	16.0%
African-Americans	72.0%	43.0%
Hispanics	77.0%	43.0%

1990 Survey of High School Behavior

One out of five students has carried a weapon at some time.

    55% Knives and razors
    24% Clubs
    21% Guns

Gangs in Will County

Black Gangster Disciple Nation
Chicago Players
Cobra Stones
El Rukns
Gangster Disciples
Insane Unknown
Latin Counts
Latin Disciples
Latin Kings
Moorish Americans
Outlaws
Ridgewood Rebels
School Yard Crips
Vicelords
4 Corner Hustlers

Why People Join Gangs

- Identity or recognition
- Protection
- Fellowship and Brotherhood
- Intimidation
- Money

Latin Kings

Means "Brown Prince of Darkness"
Racially Mixed (Majority Latino)
Colors: Black and gold
Emblems: Cross, 5-pointed star, 5 dots,
3-pointed crown
Left Representation
Allies: Vice Lords
Foes: Black Gangster Disciples

Vice Lords

Racially Mixed (Black and Hispanic)
Colors: Black and Red
Emblems: 5-pointed star, pyramid
with a top hat, cane and
white gloves, Playboy bunny
head, dice on 7 or 11, $ sign
Left Representation
Allies: EL Rukns, Latin Kings
Foes: Black Gangster Disciples

Vocabulary

Kids – *Heroin*
Tee-Tee – *Cocaine*
Mr. X – *Dynamite*
Gemini – *Communicate*
All is one – *Used by Disciples*
Gang banger – *Gang member*
Home boy – *Friend*

Red – *Marijuana*
Blackness – *Gun power*
Fingers – *Knife*
Aries – *Latin*
Get down – *Fight*
Hood – *Neighborhood*

Graffiti

– To establish territory
– To show hate for rival gang
– To glorify gangs

CLASS 17

IV. REVIEW QUESTIONS

Now that you have completed readings and viewed the videotape you should answer the following questions to make sure you understand the key concepts presented.

1. What are some of the reasons that children in the U.S. are neglected and at risk?

2. Discuss some of the objectives of the Children's Defense Fund.

3. Is there a relationship between the plight of some children in the U.S. and the rise of gang participation in our cities?

4. List at least four reasons why young people join gangs.

5. Name several ways in which gang members identify themselves and their territory.

6. What are some methods that schools and communities can use to prevent or control the spread of gangs?

7. According to the article by Michael Katz, how has the development of a black underclass affected black youth in America?

V. SUGGESTED ADDITIONAL BACKGROUND MATERIALS

Children's Defense Fund Materials are available from the following address: Children's Defense Fund, 122 C Street, NW, Washington, D.C. 20001

Kozol, J. (1991). *Savage Inequalities*, Crown Publishers, New York, NY.

DEALING WITH DIVERSITY — CLASS 18
Gender Issues in the U.S: Part I

I. INTRODUCTION

This is the first of a two part segment on gender issues in the U.S. In the first class we will discuss issues concerning women. We will examine the progress they have made at various levels of the job market and how well they are faring overall econo-mically. In the second class we will take a brief look at the men's movement through a discussion of passages from Robert Bly's book, *Iron John*.

Our special guest for the first class is Ms. Susan Catania who is currently a government consultant. Catania will share many interesting insights from her tenure as a member of the Illinois State Legislature. She has been a catalyst for many of the changes in the legislation that now protect and expand the rights of women in Illinois.

As you view this lesson be sure to note the changes in percentages of women in the work place as well as the percentages showing female participation in selected fields. How have these changes impacted the nature of the family in the 1990's and beyond? Do the personal experiences of Catania and members of the class support this claim that conditions for women have greatly improved over the last 20 years?

 Before you watch the videotape for this lesson:
READ: 7: "Gender Stereotypes and Roles" in *The Meaning of Difference*, pages 81-96.
29: "The Mismeasure of Woman" in *The Meaning of Difference*, pages 336-353.

II. VIDEO INSERTS

The video insert for this class is an interview with Dr. Pauline Treichler, Professor of Sociology at the University of Illinois Champaign- Urbana, and co-author of the book, *The Feminist Dictionary*. As you watch this interview consider the following questions.

A. Why was there a need for the development of a feminist dictionary?

B. What is the current stage of the feminist movement as described by Dr. Treichler?

III. GRAPHICS

 At this stage we suggest you watch the videotape. The graphics you will see on the screen are reproduced below to save you the trouble of copying them down. You might like to add your own comments as you watch the tape.

Women in the Labor Force

Year	Number (1000)	% Females	% of Labor Force
1900	5,319	18.8	18.3
1920	8,637	21.4	20.4
1940	12,845	25.4	24.3
1960	23,268	37.8	32.5
1980	45,611	51.6	42.0
1990	56,554	57.5	45.3

Women as % of All Workers

Occupation	1975	1986
Dental Assistant	100.0	99.0
Registered Nurse	97.0	94.3
Telephone Operator	93.3	87.9
Elem. School Teacher	85.4	85.2
Librarian	81.1	85.9
Airline Pilot	0	1.5
Dentist	1.8	4.4
Lawyer/Judge	7.1	18.1
Physician	12.0	17.6
Economist	13.1	39.3

Occupations of Women

Occupation	1984	1987	1990
Mangerial and Professional	22.5	24.4	26.2
Technical, Sales, Admin. Support	45.6	46.1	44.4
Service	18.7	18.1	17.1
Precision Production and Repair	2.4	2.3	2.2
Operators, Laborers	9.6	9.0	8.5
Farming, Forestry	1.2	1.1	1.1

Mothers Participating in Labor Force		
Mother with Children		
Year	Under 18 Years	6 to 17 Years	Under 6 Years
1955	27.0%	38.4%	18.2%
1965	35.0	45.7	25.3
1975	47.4	54.8	38.9
1985	62.1	69.9	53.5
1990	66.7	74.7	58.2

Weekly Earnings of Full-Time Women Workers		
Major Occupation	1990 Per Week	% Man's Salary
Executive	485	69.9
Professional	534	65.4
Technicians	417	73.2
Sales	292	57.8
Clerical	332	75.5
Service	230	71.8
All Occupations	348	71.8

Median Income – 1989

Years of School	Median Income		Women's Income as % of Men's
	Women	Men	
Elementary:			
8 or less years	$11,712	$17,204	68
High School:			
1 to 3 years	13,222	20,623	64
4 years	16,865	25,859	65
College:			
1 to 3 years	20,764	30,406	68
4 years	25,908	36,845	70

CLASS 18

IV. REVIEW QUESTIONS

Now that you have completed the readings and watched the videotape you should answer the following questions to make sure you understand the key concepts presented.

1. How has the percentage of women in the work force changed over the last 20 years?

2. In what professions have women made the least and most gains over the past 20 years?

3. List some of the reasons why women get paid less even though they may have the same education and experience.

4. Discuss some of the contributions that Ms. Catania has made during her tenure in the Illinois Legislature.

5. Describe some of the difficulties Ms. Catania faced when she attempted to change the laws in the Illinois State Legislature.

6. Why do women in the nineties have difficulty in seeing themselves as feminists?

7. Explain why you would or would not support the view discussed by the author of the article "The Five Sexes."

8. Carol Tarvis states in her article that she believes it is possible for females and males to be treated equally in our society. State whether you agree or disagree with her ideas.

V. SUGGESTED ADDITIONAL BACKGROUND MATERIALS

Hooks, B. (1984). *Feminist Theory, from Margin to Center*. South End Press. Boston, MA.

Treichler, P. (1985). *The Feminist Dictionary*, Pandora Press, Boston, MA.

I. INTRODUCTION

This is the second class on the issue of Gender. In this segment the class engages in a free wheeling discussion. In the first part of the class there is a discussion on the men's movement focusing on Robert Bly's book, *Iron John*. The discussion then changes gears and the class really gets involved, sharing their own stories about their rites of passage in childhood and adolescence. This class discussion is one of the most engaging in the course.

Be sure to pay special attention to the variety of perspectives on gender, role and status held by students in the class. Where do we get our gender identities? How has the traditional enculturation of gender changed given the advent of the post industrial/high technology economic system?

Before you watch the videotape for this lesson:
READ: 6: "The Berdache Tradition" in *The Meaning of Difference*, pages 73-81.

II. QUOTATIONS

The following quotations from Robert Bly's "Iron John" are read during the class.

— only men can initiate men, as only women can initiate women. (p. 16)

— The industrial revolution, in its need for office and factory workers, pulled fathers away from their sons and, moreover, placed the sons in compulsory schools where the teachers are mostly women. (p. 19)

— If the father inhabits the house only for an hour or two in the evenings, then women's values, marvelous as they are, will be the only values in the house. One could say that the father now loses his son five minutes after birth. (p. 20-21)

— Some women feel hurt when a man will not "express his feelings," and they conclude that he is holding back, or "telling them something" by such withholding; but it's more likely that when such a man asks a question of his chest, he gets no answer at all. (p. 68)

— If a young man now feels the need to drop out of school, there is no ritual for that, and he may easily end up shamed, or worse, in prison. (p. 80)

New Guinea custom held by 80 or so tribes:

— A boy cannot change into a man without the active intervention of the older men. A girl changes into a woman on her own, with the bodily developments marking the change; old women tell her stories and chants, and do celebrations. But with the boys, no old men, no change.

CLASS 19

III. REVIEW QUESTIONS

Now that you have completed the readings and viewed the videotape you should answer the following questions to make sure you understand the key concepts presented in this class.

1. According to Bly's *Iron John,* what is it that most males have lost in their sense of self?

2. According to Bly what are the possible long term benefits to society as a result of the men's movement?

3. Do both men and women share the same rites of passage to adulthood? In what ways do they differ?

4. Describe how gender identity is changing in contemporary society?

5. Briefly discuss the difference in how some Native American cultures view gender as compared to other cultures.

IV. SUGGESTED ADDITIONAL BACKGROUND MATERIALS

Bly, R. (1990). *Iron John*. Vintage Books: New York

Doubiago, S. (1992). Enemy of the Mother: A Feminist Response to the Men's Movement. *Ms. Magazine*. V2 N5, pp.82-86. (Mar-Apr)

Pittman, F. (1992). Why the Men's Movement Isn't So Funny. *Psychology Today*. V25 N1 p.84. (Jan-Feb)

I. INTRODUCTION

This is the first of two classes that will examine some of the many issues involving sexuality within the U.S. In the first class we have two special guests from the Illinois Gay and Lesbian Task Force who will discuss a variety of issues dealing with being a homosexual in our society. In the second class we will explore the political side of the issue through the experiences of two individuals involved with the organization, "The Forgotten Boy Scouts". They will also share some of their own personal histories as a result of their sexual orientation.

Our guests for this class are Jovita Baber and Vernon Huls who represent the Illinois Gay and Lesbian Task Force. They will discuss a variety of issues confronting men's and women's sexual orientation in our society, including the increase of violence against gays, political activism, and the changing self identity of gays/lesbians. Baber will discuss her work with an organization called SCAN's (Statewide Campus Action Network); make sure that you understand the purpose and function of this organization. There is also a very candid discussion on stereotypes that surround the gay/lesbian experience. Are your stereotypes similar to those of the class? If so, does the class discussion moderate your view somewhat on this subject?

There are two other important issues discussed to which you need to pay special attention. The first has to do with the heterosexual view of female/lesbian sexuality and its inherent misconceptions. The second issue relates to power – the power of homophobia exercised over homosexuals, and the empowerment homosexuals experience when they undergo the arduous process of "coming out."

Before you watch the videotape for this lesson:
READ: 10: "Homosexuality: A Social Phenomenon" in *The Meaning of Difference*, pages 120-129.

II. GRAPHICS

At this stage we suggest you watch the videotape. The graphics you will see on the screen are reproduced below to save you the trouble of copying them down. You might like to add your own comments as you watch the tape.

Anti-Gay/Lesbian Episodes Reported to Gay and Lesbian Victim Service Agencies					
Metro Boston	37	84	147	209	465%
Metro Chicago	149	179	198	210	41%
Metro Minneapolis/St. Paul	24	48	112	338	1308%
Metro New York	289	308	507	592	105%
Metro San Francisco	198	330	425	473	139%
Total	**697**	**949**	**1,389**	**1,822**	**161%**
% Increase over previous year		**36%**	**46%**	**31%**	

CLASS 20

III. REVIEW QUESTIONS

Now that you have completed the readings and viewed the videotape for this class you should answer the following questions to make sure you understand the key concepts presented.

1. What are some of the difficulties that gays/lesbians face when they have open relationships in society?

2. Given the discussions presented in class what are some of the current theories to explain why the issue of sexual orientation of gays/lesbians has surfaced in the last 20 years?

3. What are some of the most common stereotypes generated about homosexuality?

4. Discuss why you believe the instances of violence against gays/lesbians have increased in recent years?

5. Describe the role that the lesbian movement has played in changing the sexual relationships of gay men in the 1990's?

6. According to Baber what are some of the major differences between the gay and lesbian culture?

7. According to the article "Homosexuality: A Social Phenomenon," how has the definition of homosexuality changed in the last 200 years?

IV. SUGGESTED ADDITIONAL BACKGROUND MATERIALS

Eichberg, R. (1990). *Coming Out: An Act of Love.* A Blume Book: New York.

Evans, N. and Wall, V. eds. (1991). Gays, Lesbians, and Bisexuals on Campus. *Association for Counseling and Development.* Alexandria, VA.

Gessen, M. and McGowan, D. (1992). Raiders of the Gay Gene: Scientists Trying to Prove that Sexuality is Biologically Determined Are the New Media Darlings. *The Advocate.* March 24. N599 pp.60-63.

Holden, C. (1992). Twin Study Links Genes to Homosexuality. *Science.* V255 N5040 p.33.

DEALING WITH DIVERSITY — CLASS 21
Sexual Orientation Issues in the U.S: Part 2

I. INTRODUCTION

This is the second class on the topic of sexual orientation in the U.S. In this class we will focus on the experiences of our two guests. The first guest is Mr. Schwitz who is a member of the Forgotten Boy Scouts, a nationwide organization that represents males who have been ejected from the Boy Scouts of America Inc (BSA). This organization is challenging the rights of the BSA to continue what they consider to be discriminatory practices against gays. The second guest, Mr. Shore, relates his experiences with the establishment of the Oakland Men's Group and their activities in the Oakland, California area. Both guests should help you understand something of the culture and experiences of individuals in our society whose sexual preferences have directly affected their opportunity for equity and equality.

 Before you watch the videotape for this lesson:
READ: 11: "Development of Gay, Lesbian, and Bisexual Identities" in *The Meaning of Difference*, pages 130-136.

 At this stage we suggest you watch the videotape.

II. REVIEW QUESTIONS

Now that you have completed the readings and viewed the videotape for this class you should answer the following questions to make sure you understand the key concepts presented.

1. Discuss why organizations like the Forgotten Boy Scouts and the Oakland Men's Group have come into existence?

2. List some of the arguments that BSA Inc. have advanced for the elimination of gays as members of the BSA Inc.

3. Why do the Forgotten Boy Scouts feel it is illegal for the BSA Inc. to dis criminate against gays?

4. How do you think the forces of culture impact on our interpretation of what is normal and what is abnormal?

5. Contrast the difference and similarities in Gay, Lesbian and Bisexual Identity as described in the article by Heidi Levine and Nancy J. Evans.

III. SUGGESTED ADDITIONAL BACKGROUND MATERIALS

Dynes, W. eds. (1990). *Encyclopedia of Homosexuality*. Garland Press. New York.

Vicinus, M. et. al. (1989). *Hidden From History: Reclaiming the Gay and Lesbian Past*. NAL Books. New York.

Hochswender, W. (1992). Boy Scouts Learn Levi's Don't Fit; A Policy on Gay Members Dooms A Donation. *The New York Times*. June 2, V141 p.84.

DEALING WITH DIVERSITY — CLASS 22
Ability Issues in the U.S.

I. INTRODUCTION

This class focuses on one of the largest groups in our society and yet one that has one of the lowest visibilities in our culture. The group is the disabled, and their numbers total over 30 million individuals who represent all ethnicities, cultures, ages, and incomes in our society. Our special guest for this class is Lenda Hunt, Director of Options Center for Independent Living, in Kankakee, Illinois. When Hunt became a paraplegic as a result of an automobile accident, she became a determined advocate for promoting the rights of the disabled. She discusses a variety of issues that face the disabled including the issues of accessibility, the culture of the disabled, social interaction problems and economic problems.

Hunt argues that the disabled are the group subjected to the most discrimination in society. She also discusses what is necessary for society to begin to accept the disabled and provide them the same opportunities that every citizen in our country deserves.

 Before you watch the videotape for this lesson:
READ: "I am Legally Blind" in *The Meaning of Difference*, page 224.

II. VIDEO INSERT

The video interview for this class was with Mr. Hiram Zayas, Director of Rehab Consulting in Chicago, Illinois. As you watch this interview consider the following questions:

A. When you see Zayas for the first time what thoughts immediately come to your mind? After the interview was over did your feelings change?

B. Why is access so important in the lives of the disabled?

C. According to Zayas the disabled are just becoming aware of their political and economic potential; what are the likely outcomes of their increased participation.

D. How would you describe Mr. Zayas? In what way would you consider him "exceptional?"

E. What are some of the benefits that the disabled employee brings to the workplace?

 At this stage we suggest you watch the videotape.

III. REVIEW QUESTIONS

Now that you have completed the readings and reviewed the video tape for this class you should answer the following questions to make sure you understand the key concepts presented.

1. Why is the terminology we use to discuss people with disabilities so important for both the disabled as well as the able?

2. List several reasons why access is a critical issue for the disabled.

3. Discuss what benefits the disabled can contribute to society, as employees, tax payers, and citizens.

4. According to Hunt when and how should a person help disabled people when they encounter them in a public situation?

5. Define the acronym T.A.B. and discuss its significance to all of us.

6. In the personal account "I am Legally Blind" discuss the dilemma experienced by the author.

IV. SUGGESTED ADDITIONAL BACKGROUND MATERIALS

Bursuck, W., et. al. (1989). Nationwide Survey of Post Secondary Education Services for Students with Learning Disabilities. *Exceptional Children*. November V56 N3, pp.236-246.

Lerner, J. (1988). *Learning Disabilities*. Houghton Mifflin Company. Boston, Mass.

McKee, B. (1991). What You Must Do for the Disabled. *Nation's Business*. December V79 N12 pp.36-40.

For more specific information about the American Disabilities Act contact:

Equal Employment Opportunity Commission
1801 L Street, NW
Washington, D.C. 20507

Architectural and Transportation Barriers Compliance Board
1111 18th Street, NW
Suite 501
Washington, D.C. 20036

DEALING WITH DIVERSITY — CLASS 23
Hate Groups in the U.S.

I. INTRODUCTION

In this class we will focus on what society has labeled as "hate groups". You will have the opportunity to see and listen to a leader of one of these groups. Arthur J. Jones is the National Chairman of the America First Committee, an organization which claims to be associated with the earlier organization that was founded in 1940 by a group of prominent American patriots which included Colonel Charles A. Lindberg.

Arthur Jones was a member of the NS White People's Party and was that party's candidate for Mayor of Milwaukee in 1976. More recently he has run for Congress in the 3rd District in 1991.

The America First Committee's Preamble is stated as follows:

Preamble

We, the members and supporters of the America First Committee assembled this day of June 8, 1980, do hereby pledge ourselves to the following ten (10) propositions:

1. That all men are not created equal in mind or body and that this natural inequality among men and races is of Divine origin

2. That the natural law governing all human life is based in the maintenance of racial integrity and genetic heredity

3. That the basis for all social development in human affairs is the preservation of the family, property and respect for all duly constituted authority

4. That it is the duty of the state to safeguard the lives and property of its citizens; to provide avenues for honorable men to provide for themselves the necessities for a decent human life

5. That the basis for all prosperity in a society lies in the talents and productivity of its people

6. That a free and sovereign people are the masters not the servants of money in their own land

7. That the purpose of education is to preserve for future generations the highest elements of white, western culture

8. That in foreign affairs, the rights of a free people are not subservient to any foreign states, alliances, or international bodies

9. That it is the duty of the state to provide for its own self- defense; and it is the right of a free people to keep and bear arms to defend themselves against any intruder or oppressor

10. That the ideals of government for which we shall strive are Liberty without Anarchy; Law and Order without Tyranny.

As you watch this class keep in mind the aforementioned ten propositions.

Before you watch the videotape for this lesson:
READ: 22: "The Rise and Fall of Affirmative Action" in *The Meaning of Difference*, pages 272-286.
13: "Talking Past Each Other: Black and White Languages of Race" in *The Meaning of Difference*, pages 167-176.

CLASS 23

II. GRAPHICS

At this stage we suggest you watch the videotape. The graphics you will see on the screen are reproduced below to save you the trouble of copying them down. You might like to add your own comments as you watch the tape.

Hate Groups in the U.S.A.

Group	1990	1991
Ku Klux Klan	69	97
Neo-Nazi	160	203
Other	44	46
Total	**273**	**346**

Location of Hate Groups

Ku Klux Klan
Florida and North Georgia

Neo-Nazis, Skinheads
Northeast
Southern California
Chicago
Detroit

III. REVIEW QUESTIONS

Now that you have completed the readings and reviewed the videotape for this class you should answer the following questions to make sure you understand the key concepts presented.

1. What was the origin behind the development of the America First Committee?

2. Describe the significance and importance of the uniform that Arthur Jones was wearing.

3. Given the goals and objectives of the America First Committee what in your opinion could this organization contribute to our society?

4. Interpret and explain Mr. Jones' use of the term "retards" in reference to certain groups of people.

5. Explain why Mr. Jones believes Jews have been one of the major reasons for the decline of white people in America and around the world.

6. Why does Mr. Jones fear interracial marriage in society?

7. How do you think Arthur Jones would react to the article "The Rise and Fall of Affirmative Action"? How has this article affected your opinion on this subject?

8. Discuss the differences between race and ethnicity as these terms are used by the various cultural groups within American society.

IV. SUGGESTED ADDITIONAL BACKGROUND MATERIALS

Cooper, M. (1989). The Growing Danger of Hate Groups. *Editorial Research Reports*. May, V1 N18 pp.262-273.

Newton, M. and Newton, J. (1991). *The Ku Klux Klan: An Encyclopedia*. Garland Publishers. New York.

Nieli, R. ed. (1991). *Racial Preference and Racial Justice: The New Affirmative Action Controversy*. Ethics and Public Policy Center. Washington, D.C.

America First Committee
P.O. Box 6139
Chicago, Illinois 60680

Klanwatch Project
Southern Poverty Law Center
400 Washington Avenue
Montgomery, Alabama 36104

DEALING WITH DIVERSITY — CLASS 24
Summary and Review of the Teleclass: Dealing with Diversity

I. INTRODUCTION

This is the final class in the Dealing With Diversity Series. In this class we will review some of the central issues we have covered throughout the semester. In order to provide a framework for this discussion we will utilize the Social Interaction Model and its concepts to guide our efforts. We will also seek to integrate some of the various topics we have discussed this semester as well as examine some new ones.

In the first part of the class we will discuss the unique propriospects of some of our many in-class guests as well as the interviews from our video inserts. We will then examine the variety of cultural scenes we have encountered from the social interaction in the Adult Day Care Centers to the electric atmosphere created in the studio during the class with Arthur Jones from the America First Committee. In each of these situations be sure to reflect on the unique set of circumstances and issues that we explored as we sought to make sense out of these events. As the decision making component of the model is discussed try and remember what your favorite class segments were that employed some interesting examples of individual or group decision making. Finally, note the different ways in which social distance was discussed in terms of ethnic/racial, gender, SES, and sexual orientation aggregations.

Throughout this class we have attempted to bring understanding to the diversity of groups that we encounter in society. While we may not always agree with their views, our survival in this global village we call earth is dependent upon our ability to see past our differences and embrace a common humanity as brothers and sisters, who share mutual respect and dignity.

 Before you watch the videotape for this lesson:
READ: Section II: "Experiencing Difference" in *The Meaning of Difference*, pages 137-162.

 At this stage we suggest you watch the videotape.

II. REVIEW QUESTIONS

1. Discuss some of the positives and negatives associated with privilege and stigma as stated in the second framework article "Experiencing Difference."

III. SUGGESTED ADDITIONAL BACKGROUND MATERIALS

Cushner, K., et. al. (1992). *Human Diversity in Education: An Integrative Approach*. McGraw Hill. New York.

The Family of Man - The Museum of Modern Art (1955). Simon and Schuster Inc. New York.

Teaching Tolerance Materials, Southern Poverty Law Center
400 Washington Avenue, Montgomery, Alabama 36104

Fernandez-Armesto, Felipe. (1995). Mellennium: A History of the Last Thousand Years. New York: Scribner

Acculturation

The process of acquiring a second culture which is different from the one originally enculturated in.

Acquaintance

A person whom one knows only slightly.

Afrocentricity

A philosophy that seeks to regenerate the connection between the millions of Africans on the continent and in the Diaspora.

Aggregation

The voluntary clustering by race. Seating aggregation can be an index for assessing student attitudes about interracial and interethnic contact.

Association

A relationship resulting from participation in some formal or informal organization like a class or club.

Best friend

A confidant with whom one can share very personal information, a critic/advisor whose counsel is acceptable, a standard against which to measure oneself.

* ConServ

Consortium for Services to Homeless Families, Inc. which specializes in getting homeless people back into their own homes.

Cues/Clues

Context information like the props in a CS that assist the actor in presenting the appropriate range of behaviors for a given event.

Cultural Scene (CS)

The information shared by two or more people that defines some aspect of their experience. CS is closely linked to recurrent social situations. Complex social organizations, like schools, provide numerous settings that qualify as CS.

Culture

The cognitive rules for appropriate behavior (including linguistic behavior) which are learned by people as a result of being members of the same group or community and also the perceptions, skills, knowledge, values, assumptions, and beliefs which underlie overt behaviors and are themselves shared products of group membership.

Demography

The statistical study of human populations with special reference to size and density, distribution, and vital statistics.

Dialect

A form of speech characteristic of a class or region and different from the standard language in pronunciation, vocabulary, and grammatical form.

Diaspora

Any scattering or dispersion of people with a common origin, background, or beliefs.

Egocentrism

A tendency to view one's inherent qualities as superior to any other individual(s) one comes in contact with.

Enculturation

The development through the influence of parents with reinforcement by others in society of patterns of behavior in children that conform to the standards deemed appropriate by the culture (also called socialization).

Ethnic Group

A microcultural group or collectivity that shares a common history and culture, common values, behaviors, and other characteristics that cause members of the group to have a shared identity.

Ethnocentrism

A tendency to view alien cultures with disfavor and a resulting sense of inherent superiority.

Event

A specific type of CS that involves people in purposeful activities acting on objects and interacting with each other to achieve some result.

Event Familiarity

The amount of general knowledge an individual brings to a specific CS based on his/her propriospect which is necessary for accurate prediction of the event scenario and appropriate behavior.

Fictive Kinship

The kinship-like relationship between persons not related by blood or marriage in a society, but who have come reciprocal social or economic relationship.

General Knowledge

The basic information that all humans understand like the need for food and water.

Global Village

The concept of referring to the earth's inhabitants as sharing a single interdependent community.

Idiolect

An individual's unique system of articulation. No two speakers operate a language in the "same" manner.

Macroculture

The predominant core culture of a society. Even though the US has been influenced by a number of microcultures, it is probably most characterized by its WASP traits.

Microculture

Cultures that consist of unique institutions, values, and cultural elements that are nonuniversalized and are shared primarily by members of specific cultural groups.

Marginality

The dilemma some individuals have who find they are trapped between the macrocultures they can't fully assimilate into and their own indigeneous culture that they are no longer accepted in.

Multicultural Education

A reform movement designed to change the total educational environment so that students from diverse racial and ethnic groups, both gender groups, exceptional students, and students from each social class group will experience equal education opportunities in schools, colleges, and universities. A major assumption of multicultural education is that some students, because of their particular racial, ethnic, gender, and cultural characteristics, have a better chance to succeed in educational institutions as they are currently structured than do students who belong to other groups or have different cultural and gender characteristics. (Banks, 1989)

* National Savings

The share of national product left after private consumption and government spending.

Negative Recognition

The avoidance and rejection of individuals based on their physical characteristics, dress, language, and SES.

Novice

Within the context of Event Familiarity, a beginner or neophyte lacking the specific knowledge necessary for predicting the behaviors of others and the selection of their own appropriate behaviors for the given CS.

Oppositional Frame of Reference

The subordinate minorities' strategy for protecting their identity and for maintaining boundaries between them and white Americans. (Ogbu, 1986)

Oppositional Social Identity

The subordinate minorities' perception of the experience and treatment by whites as collective and enduring oppression. (Ogbu, 1986)

Paradigm

A conceptual model that serves as a cognitive map to organize experience so that it has meaning and is comprehensible to the observer. Basic paradigms provide the core assumptions about the nature of reality and set the boundaries for intellectual discourse.

Persona

One of an individual's many identities.

Predictability

The need for humans to be able to diagnose, forecast, or anticipate events in CS.

Prejudice

Unfavorable opinion or feeling formed beforehand without knowledge, thought,
or reason.

Propriospect

The sum total of an individual's experiences that enables him/her to make himself/herself intelligible to others well enough at least to permit him/her to accomplish many of his/her purposes through them.

Proxemics

The study of personal and cultural spatial needs and their interaction with their environmental space.

Race

An invalid paradigm, developed by people to justify the different treatments accorded to different people. A variety of classification systems ranging from 3 to 32 races developed to separate humans by physical and or geographic characteristics.

Racism

Any attitude, action, or institutional structure which subordinates a person or group because of their color. Racism isn't just a matter of attitudes: actions and institutional structures can also be a form of racism. Racism is different from racial prejudice, hatred, or discrimination. Racism involves having the power to carry out systematic discriminatory practices through the major institutions of our society.

Recipes

Cognitive routines established over time through repetition to meet the needs of a particular situation. A way of economizing familiar episodes into
a generalized episode.

Recognition

The acknowledgement or acceptance of another individual in any given CS.

Schemata

Cognitive representations of generic concepts. They include the attributes that constitute the concept and relationships among the attributes.

Schema

Cultural schema are then abstract concepts people hold about the social world, including ideas about persons, roles, and events.

Scripts

Information that has already been established for anticipating what is to be expected and how the individual should act based on the constraints and cues present in any given situation.

Script Shifting

The employment of a secondary script in a given context that may or may not be appropriate for the accomplishment of the primary script's intended goal.

Segregation

The separation or isolation of a race, class, or ethnic group by enforced or voluntary residence in a restricted area by barriers to social intercourse, by separate educational facilities, or by other discriminatory means.

Social Distance

The patterns of acceptance and rejection toward cultural/ethnic groups held by individuals and manifested in their social interaction decisions in a society.

Social Persona

The sum total of one's selected identities.

Socio Economic Status (SES)

An index that describes such features as residency, occupation, income, and educational level.

Specific Knowledge

The information needed to interpret and participate in events we have experienced many times. This type of detailed information allows the individual to do less processing and wondering about frequently experienced events.

Status

The combination of rights and duties in which individuals have social identities that are either ascribed or achieved.

Status Mobility System (SMS)

The socially or culturally approved strategy for getting ahead within a given population or society. It is the people's folk theory of making it or getting ahead; however, the particular population defines getting ahead. (Ogbu, 1986)

T.A.B.

The Temporarily Able-Bodied. A term that references the fact that all able-bodied humans run the risk of becoming disabled at some time during their life.

Tracks

A subunit of a larger body of knowledge referred to as scripts. Within the script called the *classroom*, there are a variety of subunits called tracks like: the homeroom, the study hall, and the academic classes. Each track has its own unique set of events that separate it from other tracks that make up the *classroom* script.

Understanding

The individual's ability to interpret the CS and activate the appropriate script/recipes to respond within the range of socially acceptable behavior.

W.A.S.P.

White Anglo-Saxon Protestant

Wave Theory

A migration theory that suggests that in certain migration patterns the first group to relocate is composed of high level officials in government and the military, the well educated, and the urban elite; the second wave is composed of low-level officials, less educated merchants, and those seeking to be reunited with their families who have already left; the third wave brings the rural poor, the farmers, and the least educated.

* Terms taken from Annual Edition, *Social Problems 91/92*, Instructor's Resource Guide.

UNDERSTANDING SOCIAL INTERACTION IN CULTURALLY DIVERSE SETTINGS

J.Q. Adams
Western Illinois University

My primary teaching responsibilities at Western Illinois University involve instructing graduate teaching majors in the area of educational psychology, multicultural education, and alternatives to traditional educational practices. Given the dramatic demographic changes within the state of Illinois and across the nation, it is incumbent upon Colleges of Education, as well as other disciplines, to prepare students who can successfully understand and participate in the culturally diverse settings. In order to teach these skills, I have developed a social interaction model (SIM) and theory that breaks down the primary components of individual and group social interaction characteristics in a variety of cultural settings or scenes.

The SIM and theory have four major components: the ego, the cultural scene, decision making, and event familiarity. Each of these components helps students to understand the complexities of social interaction in society and in the classroom. The model also helps the students to understand their own interaction styles and cultural backgrounds and provides practical strategies to enhance their ability to become more effective participants in culturally diverse settings.

The Individual or Ego

Each ego or individual has developed his or her own unique propriospect or personal culture which is the result of enculturation. Goodenough (1971) states that propriospect embraces an individual's cognitive and affective ordering of his experiences which include:

The various standards for perceiving, evaluating, believing, and doing what he attributes to other persons as a result of his experiences of their actions and admonitions. By attributing standards to others, he makes sense of their behavior and is able to predict it to a significant degree. By using what he believes to be their standards for him as a guide for his own behavior, he makes himself intelligible to them and can thereby influence their behavior well enough, at least to permit him to accomplish many of his purposes through them. (p. 36)

The problem that certain ethnic group(s)/culturally different students(s) (EG/CDS) encounter is that their primary culture is often foreign to the mainstream, operating culture of the anglicized schools in which they must interact and to the anglicized teachers from whom they must learn. By anglicized I am referring to the Euroethnic/WASP cultural dominance of the U.S. educational system in which the vast majority of instructors are Euroethnic. This idea of personal culture may be linked to recent work on cognitive knowledge structures called schemas. In discussing their schema approach, Schank and Abelson (1977) state that, "People know how to act appropriately because they have knowledge about the world they live in." (p. 36) They go on to describe the two classes of knowledge that humans recognize: general knowledge and specific knowledge. General knowledge is that basic information that all humans understand, such as the need for water and food. Specific knowledge, on the other hand, is used to interpret and participate in events we have been through many times. This type of detailed specific knowledge allows the individual to do less processing and wondering about frequently experienced events. Therefore, if we assume that Goodenough's (1965) contentions are accurate, EG/CDS face a daily dilemma of reordering their "recipes" or what Schank and Abelson (1977) call <u>scripts</u>, so as to make sense of and perform the new rules of operating behavior competently enough to achieve their goals.

Each ego also processes an individual idiolect, as Goodenough (1965) again reminds us: "No two speakers of what we regard as the 'same' language actually operate with identical systems and articulation of systems." (p. 8)

This, of course, is compounded when a setting is multicultural or multiethnic with several language and dialect possibilities likely to be in operation. Given the demographic changes occurring in this nation, most colleges and universities already fit this culturally diverse description.

Both a person's propriospect and his or her idiolect are reflective of the resources available through his or her (or the parents'/guardians') socioeconomic status (SES). SES, in this instance, is being used as an index that describes such features as residence, occupation, income, and educational level. These SES factors contribute either more positively or negatively to the performance level of competencies an individual possesses for any given event. These competencies or skills are performed in a manner that would fall somewhere on the continuum between novice and expert.

The Cultural Scene

Spradley (1972) suggests that a cultural scene is the information shared by two or more people that defines some aspect of their experience. Cultural scenes are closely linked to recurrent social situations. Complex social organizations, such as colleges and universities, provide numerous settings that qualify as cultural scenes. Within each cultural scene the individual or ego faces a range of potential interactions with the other participants present, depending on their varying roles, status, scripts, plans, and goals, and the physical constraints of the setting.

It is important to elaborate on the definitions of status and role as they will be used in the context of this chapter. Goodenough (1965), drawing on the research of Linton (1936), Merton (1957), and Hoebel (1954), described statuses as a combination of rights and duties in which individuals have social identities that are either ascribed or achieved. Goodenough maintains that statuses contain the following two properties: what legal theorists call rights, duties, privileges, powers, liabilities, and immunities and the ordered ways these are distributed in what will be called identity relationships. Rights and duties form the boundaries within which individuals in any given cultural scene are expected to confine their behavior based on their knowledge of the rules of sociocultural behavior applicable to that given situation. Goodenough (1965) provides this example:

When I am invited out to dinner, it is my hostess' right that I wear a necktie; to wear one is my duty. It is also her right that its decoration be within the bounds of decency. But she has no right as to how it shall be decorated otherwise; it is my privilege to decide this without reference to her wishes.

Goodenough goes on to state:

As for powers, they and their liability counterparts stem from privileges, while immunities result from rights and the observance of duties. (p. 3)

Social identity in Goodenough's scheme refers to that aspect of an individual that determines how one's rights and duties distribute to specific others. This identity is to be distinguished from one's personal identity which relates to the way one may express one's privileges. It is also important to note that each individual has a variety of social identities. A student, for example, can also be an older and/or younger sibling, a football player, student government president, a sorority/fraternity member, and belong to a specific church. One's rights and duties vary according to the identities one assumes, as well as the identities assumed by the other participants with whom one interacts in the cultural scene. When an EG/CDS, for example, is in the classroom, it is the instructor's right to insist that the EG/CDS participate in the classroom activities; classroom participation is the EG/CDS' duty. It is also the instructor's right to demand that the EG/CDS' classroom behavior, while participating, is within the institution's acceptable range of behavior. But the teacher has no right to tell the EG/CDS with whom they should interact within the classroom on a personal level. It is the EG/CDS' privilege to decide with whom they will develop social relationships, without regard for the instructor's wishes. Thus, the exercise of the choices of privileges expresses an individual's "sense" of identity.

Since each individual possesses a myriad of identities, we must ask, how is it that an identity is selected? As Linton (1936, p. 115) contends, some identities are ascribed while others are achieved. A person's gender and age identity in most instances are a given. An 18-year-old male has the social responsibility to represent himself as a young adult and a man. But, on the other hand, he has no obligation to reveal that he is a member of the football team or what his religious preference is. Goodenough (1965) stated that there were several considerations that govern the selection of identities. For example: (a) the individual has the qualifications for selecting identities, (b) the interaction has a direct bearing on the choice of identities by the individuals present, (c) the setting of the interaction helps determine the identity, (d) an individual has only a limited number of appropriate matching responsibilities available for any identity assumed, and (e) finally, an individual is likely to have more than one identity-relationship for each cultural scene. The sum of one's selected identities is referred to as the "social persona" in the cultural scenes interaction.

Combining Spradley (1972) and Goodenough's (1965) theoretical approach leads to the proposal that in each possible cultural scene the identity relationships created among individuals have their corresponding specific allocation of rights and duties. The reciprocal agreement of these rights and duties constitutes a status relationship. Status relationships elaborate on the differences in this relationship between minorities and majorities and/or successful/unsuccessful students. In summary, a culturally ordered system of social relationships, then, is composed (among other things) of identity relationships, status relationships, and finally the ways they are mutually distributed. Goodenough describes an individual's role as the aggregate of its composite statuses. In other words, it would be equivalent to all the duty-statuses and right-statuses for a given identity. Each individual identity will differ in some ways, with some having greater privileges and possibilities for gratification than others. Therefore, each individual identity has a different place or function in the social system in which he or she resides. In order to sum up this discussion on status and roles, Cicourel (1974) states:

Statuses, like general rules or policies, require recognition and interpretation during which interacting participants must elicit and search appearances for relevant information about each other. Role-taking and role-making require that the actor articulate general rules or policies (norms) with an emergent (constructed) action scene in order to find the meaning of one's own behavior or that of some other. (p. 29)

Cicourel's statement is especially apt in the context of this paper since the individuals under scrutiny are EG/CDS who are oftentimes unaware of the full range of nuances involved in recognizing the status and/or the roles of the more anglicized faculty, staff, and students. This, of course, also applies to the anglicized students' ability to recognize and accurately construct the status and roles of EG/CD faculty, staff, and students in their enculturative settings as well as to assess what their status and roles are in the acculturative scenes of the anglicized school.

Each individual or ego reacts to a given setting or cultural scene based on his or her own individual enculturative experiences, among other things. For most situations, "schemata," or "scripts," have already been established for what is to be expected and how the individual should act based on the constraints and cues present in any given situation. Recipes can be thought of as cognitive routines established over time through repetition to meet the needs of a particular situation. Schank and Abelson describe scripts as a way of economizing familiar episodes into a generalized standard episode. In other words, scripts handle typical everyday situations.

There are numerous cultural scenes and settings within the college/university ranging from the academic classroom, to the residence hall, to extracurricular activities, and to the University Union. Each specific cultural scene in the school context has its own unique set of constraints and participants.

The Decision-Making Process

Given the constraints of the various cultural scenes EG/CDS encounter within the college/university, the EG/CDS are constantly faced with such decisions as to where, when, and with whom they should interact. While some cultural scenes within the college/university, such as the classroom, have pre-selected or tracked populations and perhaps fixed seating requirements, other settings such as the residence halls, dining rooms, or the hallways outside classrooms, are more open and feature a wider range of peers with whom one can interact. Since these cultural scenes are reoccurring situations or events, the participants have developed recipes or scripts to govern their behavior in them. Events according to Nelson (1986) are more of a macro order; they involved people in purposeful activities acting on objects and interacting with each other to achieve some result.

Let us take, for example, a script we will call the CLASSROOM. According to Schank and Abelson (1977), all participants in the classroom would bring with them specific knowledge and detail about the standard events that occur in the anglicized classroom, including information about the various roles (instructor, students, graduate assistant), props (instructor's desk, student's desk, books, homework, chalkboards), and event tracks (lecture, laboratory, exam). Since much of what takes place in the classroom frequently occurs in a specific "expectable" order, we can assume that the participants are familiar with the corresponding repertoire of behaviors necessary for a high level of social competence in that setting. However, assuming that in some cases the EG/CDS' original script of the classroom will possess some cultural differences as a result of their different enculturative experiences, modifications will have to be made in their CLASSROOM script in order to accommodate the specific knowledge necessary to perform in the mainstream anglicized classroom. Some students will bring more deficit scripts into the classroom than other students whose high school, community college, or other experiences may be more transferable. Thus, one might propose that initially, at least, the EG/CDS utilize the general knowledge from their EG/CD CLASSROOM script as a foundation for the development of their new anglicized CLASSROOM script.

Within this larger body of knowledge we call the CLASSROOM script are specific tracks such as the lecture hall, the laboratory, the practicum, and the various academic classes (math, science, English), each with its own unique set of events that separates it from the other tracks that make up the CLASSROOM script. Schank and Abelson also point out that there are ways more than one script can be active at once. Take for example a situation where "student Alpha," an anglicized student, asks "student Beta," an EG/CDS, if he is going to the soccer match after classes. The question asked by Alpha departs from the situational CLASSROOM script and activates the personal FRIENDSHIP script of both participants. This type of script shifting is not unusual; however, for the novice EG/CDS, the cross-cultural differences in the anglicized FRIENDSHIP script may create some cognitive dissonance, especially for the newly arrived international student or the more ethnically traditional EG/CDS. On the other hand, their more acculturated peers, who have been in anglicized situations longer, have had more time to acquire the nuances of the anglicized FRIENDSHIP script. This greater knowledge of anglicized culture will enable them to demonstrate a higher level of expertise in this event. Thus, Beta understands that Alpha's statement is really an invitation, which is a specific track of the FRIENDSHIP script, and responds appropriately, "Yes, I am planning to go to the game. Would you like to sit together?" Another problem with this form of script-shifting is that the teacher may interpret this brief communication between Alpha and Beta as a breach in the classroom rules and exact some form of discipline and/or penalty if it continues. Script-shifting is sometimes employed as a strategy by the student to gain attention from one's peers or as an expression of not understanding what is going on in the classroom script. A discussion of event familiarity and degrees of expertise will be presented in the next section.

EG/CDS who come from less anglicized cultural settings than the predominantly anglicized college/universities face the obstacles of developing new schema to support the recipes or scripts necessary for appropriate behavior in any given event. Underlying the need for expertise in script interaction is the need for understanding. Schank and Abelson state:

> *Understanding then is a process by which people match what they see and hear to pre-stored groupings of actions that they have already experienced. New information is understood in terms of old information. By this view, man is seen as a processor that only understands what it has previously understood. (p. 67)*

Understanding allows an individual to not only be predictive in nature but also have the ability to adapt to events with which he or she does not have previous experience. This point is critical. Effective teaching in our culturally diverse classrooms requires that we should take the time to make sure our students understand and can operate the necessary scripts to give them the best opportunity for success.

Event Familiarity—From Novice to Expert

Given that EG/CDS bring into the anglicized school scripts that were based on the social-cultural knowledge of their own enculturative experience in their primary culture, and given that the cultural scenes they face in anglicized settings are often very different from the cultural scenes in their culture of origin, each EG/CDS can be expected to respond to each new cultural scene with differing degrees of experience or expertise. Fivush and Slackman (1986) state:

> We believe that even the simplest action routine is imbued with social meaning. The social meaning defines not only what this particular event is about, but also how it fits into the larger cultural context. (p. 72)

We can assume, therefore, that even though EG/CDS will have scripts from which to access general knowledge about the classroom and academic success, they may lack the specific knowledge necessary for accurate prediction and appropriate behavior.

Slackman, Hudson, and Fivush (1986) discuss this phenomenon as "event familiarity." Borrowing from the research of Taylor and Winkler (1980), they describe four phases of expertise in adults which I believe would also apply to college-age students: (a) the rudimentary (or episodic) phase where knowledge of an example is used to make inferences about other apparently similar instances. An example of this would be EG/CDS making assumptions about what happens in anglicized schools based on a single experience of registering for classes; (b) the stereotypic phase where only the most representative attributes are featured. In the school example prototypical actions such as reading, writing, and studying are characteristic of most schools anywhere; (c) the relative expert phase where greater emphasis is placed on inconsistencies; and finally, (d) the automatic, or "mindless" phase. Thus, when EG/CDS go to predominantly anglicized colleges/universities, they would automatically know what to do in any cultural scene without necessarily being aware of the steps in the process.

Summary

In this chapter I sought to develop a theoretical model of social interaction in culturally diverse settings. This model contains four major components: (a) the individual or ego, (b) the cultural scene, (c) the decision-making process, and (d) the event familiarity range from novice to expert.

Each of these components is based upon the premise that culture is a kind of knowledge individuals acquire through the memory of personal experiences and episodes. Cognitive theorists such as Anderson (1980), Schank and Abelson (1977), and Nelson (1986), have developed a script theory through which to study events. Events involve people who are acting on objects and interacting with each other in purposeful activities to achieve some results. The events are often organized around goals and are usually made up of smaller units or episodes, each with its own schema. Scripts refer to an ordered sequence of actions appropriate to a particular spatial-temporal context and organized around a goal.

Scripts specify the actors, actions, and props used to carry out these goals within specified circumstances.

The specific circumstances in this paper are referred to as cultural scenes as defined by Spradley (1972) and include the information shared by two or more people and explain some aspect of their experiences. Cultural scenes are closely linked to recurrent social situations. Thus, the scripts developed for these scenes should allow the actors to predict what the appropriate behavioral and communicative responses are in these settings. Since the social-cultural knowledge of EG/CDS' enculturative experience often differs from that of anglicized students, the scripts that EG/CDS have for the various cultural scenes may be too general in nature to provide them with the specific anglicized knowledge needed to interact appropriately. This would be especially true in the predominant Euro-American classroom.

According to this model, the level of event familiarity that EG/CDS possess influences the kind of decision-making they are likely to exhibit, given the constraints of the situation. EG/CDS who have developed more anglicized classroom scripts are more likely to be academically successful than those who have more traditional cultural scripts and thus are more likely to maintain their more anglicized classroom scripts. The development of anglicized scripts suggests that the individuals possess social interaction skills that have reached either the relative expert or automatic stage, while their more traditional peers possess anglicized social interaction skills at the rudimentary or the stereotypic stage. The implications for these levels of expertise are twofold: (a) those students who have reached the relative expert or automatic phase continue to become more proficient in their social interaction skills each time they use them, and (b) these students have the advantage of utilizing their academic success to assist them in reaching their career and/or social goals.

References

Anderson, J. R. (1980). *Cognitive psychology and its implications*. San Francisco: W. H. Freeman.

Cicourel, A. V. (1974). *Cognitive sociology*. New York: The Free Press.

Fivush, R., & Slackman, E. A. (1986). The acquisition and development of scripts. In K. Nelson (Ed.), *Event knowledge.* (pp. 71-96). Hillsdale, NJ: Lawrence Erlbaum Associates.

Goodenough, W. H. (1965). Rethinking status and role. In M. Banton (Ed.), *The relevance of models for social anthropology* (pp. 1-14). London: Tavistock.

Goodenough, W. H. (1971). *Culture, language, and society*. Reading, MA: Addison-Wesley.

Hoebel, A. E. (1954). *The law of primitive man*. Cambridge, MA: Harvard University Press.

Linton, R. (1936). *The study of man*. New York: Appleton-Century Crofts.

Merton, R. K. (1957). *Social theory and social structure.* (rev. ed.). New York: Free Press.

Nelson, K. (1986). *Event knowledge.* Hillsdale, NJ: Lawrence Erlbaum Associates.

Schank, R. C., & Abelson, R. P. (1977). *Scripts, plans, goals and understanding.* Hillsdale, NJ: Lawrence Erlbaum.

Slackman, S. A., Hudson, J. A., & Fivush, R. (1986). Actions, actors, links, and goals: The structure of children's event representation. In K. Nelson (Ed.), *Event knowledge.* (pp. 47-69). Hillsdale, NJ: Lawrence Erlbaum Associates.

Spradley, J. P. (1972). *Culture and cognition: Rules, maps, and plans.* San Francisco: Chandler.

Taylor, S. E., & Winkler, J. D. (1980). *The development schemas.* Paper presented at the meeting of the American Psychological Association, Montreal, Canada.

Instructional Developer .... David Ainsworth

Producer/Director .... Tony Labriola

Audio Supervisor .... Jack Mulder

Video Engineers .... Ed Flowers
BobWhite
Tom Sauch
Larry Lewis
Barb McLennan

Electronic Typography and Study Guide design .... Jacquie Hemingway

Electronic Paintbox .... Leone Middleton

Production Assistants .... Renard Thomas
Rochelle Wolf
Karl Rademacher

Produced by
Communications Services .... Gary Fisk, Director

A division of the
Center for Extended Learning and
Communications Services .... Ralph Kruse, Executive Director